Knitting Things

For children aged 8 and over

Knitting Things

Rae Compton and Michael Harvey

text illustrations by Moira Buj   cover illustration by Carol Lawson

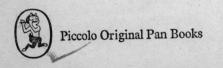

Piccolo Original Pan Books

First published 1976 by Pan Books Ltd,
Cavaye Place, London SW10 9PG
© Rae Compton and Michael Harvey 1976
ISBN 0 330 24084 6
Printed and bound in Great Britain by
Cox & Wyman Ltd, London, Reading and Fakenham

Contents

1 Preparing things

So you want to knit. Right, let's not waste any time. Luckily, very little preparation is needed for knitting. There are just one or two things that it helps to know before you begin. We can check them over quickly and avoid running into trouble later on.

It is a good idea to put all the things you will need into a small box or bag. A polythene bag will do until you are able to knit a bag for yourself.

Things you will need
Pairs of knitting needles (for this book, only sizes 7, 8, 9 and 10 – 4.5 mm, 4 mm, 3.75 mm and 3.25 mm)

Blunt-ended wool needle	Small box of pins
Small balls of yarn	Ruler
Small pair of scissors	Measuring tape

As with any craft, you will get the best results, even as a beginner, by using the best materials. It is both easier and more satisfying if you avoid using yarn that doesn't knit evenly and makes perfectly good stitches look crooked. It is also easier to learn with good needles that are designed by the manufacturer to help the person using them.

Knitting needles
Bright coloured needles look gay, but they bend and break easily. Although they look less interesting,
by far the best needles to use are those made of specially strong plastic or of plain grey metal – 'anodized aluminium', which is

simply a light metal specially treated so that it will not mark your work as you knit. Needles of this type have been carefully designed: the tip is shaped to help you as you knit and to avoid splitting the yarn, making the work difficult. Always buy a make that is named, such as Abel Morral or Milward, and you will know that experimentation and knowledge of knitting have gone into the making of them.

Needles are made in many different thicknesses. The thickest is size or number 000 and the finest or thinnest is size or number 14. The needles that are most often used are the middle sizes, numbers 8, 9 and 10. The size you will need will depend on the thickness of yarn you are going to knit, but we will look at this later.

Although needle sizes are now metric, so many people still have old needles and use patterns printed before metrication that we have kept to the old numbering system in this book. Here is a table which gives the metric equivalent of each of the old numbered sizes from thinnest to thickest.

Table of needle sizes

before metrication (number)	metric size (mm)
14	2
13	2.25
12	2.75
11	3
10	3.25
9	3.75
8	4
7	4.5
6	5
5	5.5
4	6
3	6.5
2	7
1	7.5
0	8
00	9
000	10

Pairs of needles also come in three different lengths. To start with, use 30-cm (12-inch) needles – a pair of No 8 size will be best. Longer ones are a little more difficult to use when you are learning. When you make small things, shorter, 25-cm (10-inch) needles can be used.

Yarn

Start by calling everything that you use to knit with 'yarn' and you will find that you understand what is meant. Too many

people call everything that they use 'wool'; this is silly when they are using nylon, because it is quite different.

Yarn is made in three different ways.

1 It may be made from animals' hair, cleaned and spun into a long thread: examples of this are wool, which is the fleece of the sheep; the hair of mohair goats; or the very fine, soft, fluffy hair of the angora rabbit.

2 It may be made from the fibres of plants; cotton and linen are examples.

3 It may be man-made from chemicals – for example, nylon, courtelle, acrilan, orlon, terylene, tricel and various combinations of these.

(There is also a fourth way: silkworms make and spin silk. However, silk is expensive and is only available when there is a fashion demand for it.)

Wool is the easiest to use. It is light, warm, and it has a natural elastic quality which makes stitches knitted in wool look more even than in any other type of yarn.

Cotton is gay and very useful, particularly for many things that require lots of washing, such as place mats and oven gloves.

Nylon, courtelle, terylene and tricel are all useful, although of all these nylon is the least likely to give a smooth finish when you are learning. They are hard wearing, easily available and useful for very many things.

Thickness of yarn

Yarns are available in many different thicknesses.

The most ordinary yarns are often referred to as '3 ply', '4 ply' and 'double knitting'. *Don't* make the mistake many adults make of thinking that this means that all 4-ply yarns are the same and that all double knitting is the same. This is just not so.

'4 ply' simply means that four threads are spun or twisted together into the finished yarn, and '3 ply' is made up of three threads twisted together. The basic thread can vary in thickness. Yarn that is always sold at a lower price than other yarns is usually a little thinner, although it is supposed to be the same.

Double-knitting yarn is by far the best to start with, and a good brand like Patons Double Knitting, Patons Trident Double Knitting or Patons Double Plus will make learning as easy as possible, and will knit up very nicely on your No 8 needles.

Weight of balls

The weight or size of balls does vary, but they are always marked. Today you will find that most yarn is sold in 25-gramme balls, although some are twice that size (50 grammes). As many patterns using the old measurement of ounces instead of grammes are still available, you will find that some balls of yarn are not 25 but 28.35 grammes (which is the exact equivalent of 1 ounce).

Sometimes it is possible to buy yarn in skeins, as it always used to be sold in the past. If you have a skein, then you must untie the ends very carefully, without unwinding any of the yarn. Get someone to loop it round their outstretched wrists as you wind it off the skein, loop by loop, and round your hand into a

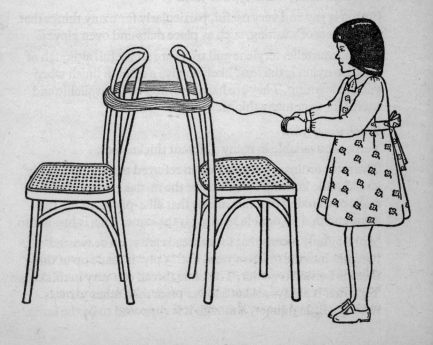

ball. When there is no one to help, you can manage by yourself if you take care. Place the skein over the backs of two chairs and move them just far enough apart to hold the skein without letting it slip down. Then your hands are free to take the end of the yarn and unwind the yarn off the chairs, one loop at a time, and make it into a ball wound round your hands.

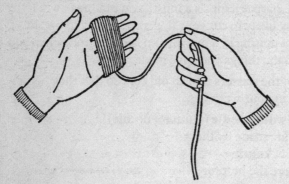

Oddments

It is quite possible to use small, 'odd' balls that you can beg from mother or friends, but try not to use yarn that has been knitted before and is uneven. You can use this once you have learned to knit, but to begin with it is easier to have new, unused yarn that makes the stitches as even as possible. This way you can see more easily when you are right and when you are wrong.

When you buy yarn for a design that uses more than one ball, do make certain that you buy all that you need at once. Yarn is dyed in batches or 'lots' and unless you buy all the balls from one lot you may find that there is a slight but noticeable difference in colour.

Try to choose a bright colour to start knitting with. If you use very dark colours – brown, navy blue or black, for example – you won't be able to see what the stitches look like; on the other hand light colours get rather grubby as you work. The best colours are red, bright pink, orange, delphinium blue, mauve, any mid shade of green, and turquoise.

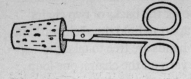

Scissors

A small pair of sharp scissors is a must. You can break wool, but you are very likely to cut your fingers if you try to break nylon instead of cutting it. You will also need scissors when you come to sew up the things you have made.

Stick the tips of the scissors into an old cork so that they don't spoil anything in your work bag.

Blunt-ended wool needle (knitter's needle)

These needles are made by the manufacturers of knitting needles. They are the best for sewing up pieces of knitting because they don't split the yarn or the stitches. You can find out how to sew up properly in Section 11.

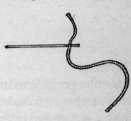

Pins

A small box of rustless pins is needed for making things up and for use when pressing articles before you sew them up or when they are finished.

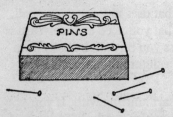

Long seams should be pinned together before being sewn so that you can be certain that they are going to fit neatly. Pinning saves you from reaching the end of the seam and finding that one edge is too long or too short, and also from getting the edges twisted.

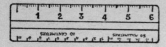

Ruler

A ruler that has both centimetres and inches marked on it is the most useful. Although the measurements in this book are given in centimetres, many patterns were printed before metrication and are therefore in inches.

Always use the ruler rather than the tape to measure knitting. Lay the work on a flat surface – not on your knee or on the arm of a chair – and measure straight up the rows (except where the instructions state otherwise, as when measuring up a sleeve seam). When an edge is curved, you must not measure round the curve – although doing this may seem to make the work 'grow' more quickly!

Measuring tape

A strong tape is needed, for measuring things that are not flat – for taking your own measurements, for example. Like the ruler, it should be marked with both centimetres and inches.

About this book

The book consists of a step-by-step guide to knitting and covers all the things you need to know.

At the end of each section there is something for you to make based on what you have learned in that chapter. This is good practice for you before you go on to the next step.

In the last section, 'Things galore', there are many more things to make. Some may use only what you have learned in one section; others may include things learned in several steps, but Section 10 *must* be read before attempting them.

Now let's get on and knit.

2 Beginning things

All knitting starts with making one slip knot.
This is how to do it.
Fold the end of the yarn over itself to form a loop.

Hold the loop between the thumb and fingers of your left hand.
Using your right hand, draw another
loop of yarn from further along nearer
the ball through the first loop.

Draw it up to form a loop that won't come loose when you let go
of it.

Take one of the pair of needles and poke it through the loop.
Draw the yarn fairly tight until the slip knot stays on the needle.

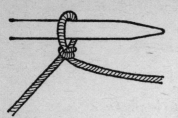

Knitting is always a matter of making a row of loops on a
needle and then working another row of loops from this first
one, using the second needle. The work grows in length because
you go on working a new row out of the one already on the
needle.

The first row that you start from is called 'casting on'.

To cast on
There are several different ways of casting on, but we only need
to learn one at the moment. This method, which is called 'the
two-needle method', or sometimes 'the English cable method',
is the way you should cast on all the 'things' in this book.

Put the needle with the slip knot on it into your left hand.

Pick up the other needle and poke the tip of it through the first
loop from the front to the back.

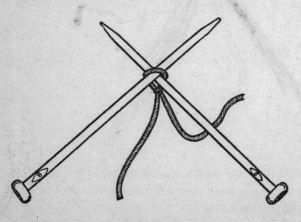

With your right hand, take the yarn that runs from the ball and bring it up and round the tip of the right-hand needle and then down between the points of the needles.

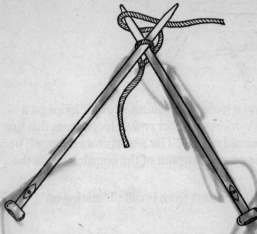

Now draw the yarn that is round the right-hand needle tip through the first loop by bringing the needle through the loop also.

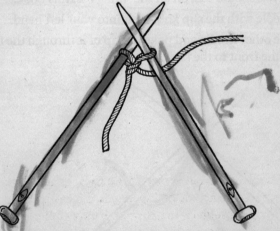

This makes a new loop and, once it is through, you can slide it back on to the needle in your left hand beside the first loop made by the slip knot.

You now have two stitches on your left-hand needle. Poke the point of the right-hand needle *between* the two stitches on the left-hand needle.

Bring the yarn up and round the tip of the right-hand needle and down between the needle points, as you did before, and again draw a loop through on to the right-hand needle.

Place this new stitch on the left-hand needle, so that you now have three loops there.

To make a new stitch, you simply put the right-hand needle

tip through between the last two stitches, make a new loop as you have done before, and slip it on to the left-hand needle.

Now there are four stitches.

Cast on another six stitches so that you have ten altogether on the left-hand needle. Now we'll learn what to do next.

If you get in a muddle, slip the stitches off and start again. The more you practise, the sooner you will be able to knit.

How to knit stitches
Put the needle with the stitches on it into your left hand.

Take the other needle in your right hand. Poke the needle without stitches into the loop of the first stitch from the front to the back.

With your right hand, bring the yarn up and over the tip of the right-hand needle and then down between the needle points.

Draw a new loop through with the right-hand needle.

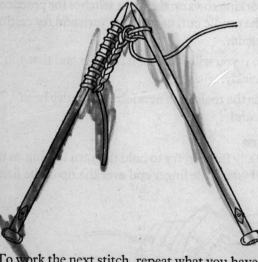

Once the new loop is made, keep it on the right-hand needle, and take the left-hand needle out of the old loop.

To work the next stitch, repeat what you have just done using the next loop on the left-hand needle. When you have done this, you will have two stitches on the right-hand needle and eight on the left-hand one. Work into each stitch in this way, making a new loop out of each stitch and keeping the new loops on the right-hand needle, until you have worked into all the stitches and have ten new stitches on the right-hand needle.

Now you have knitted one complete row. Count the stitches to see that there are still ten.

Put the needle with the stitches on it into your left hand

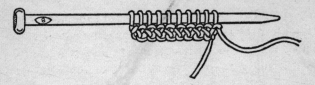

and work another row in just the same way.

Work four more rows. DO remember to change the needles round when you finish a row. The empty needle should always be in your right hand when you are ready to start a new row.

Yes, you are knitting!

You can go on working rows on these ten stitches for practice, or you can pull the needle out, unravel the yarn and try casting on and knitting again.

Each time you do it you will find that it is easier and that you can do it more quickly.

You can never use the tools for a new job as if you've been using them for years!

How to hold yarn
Before you go on any further, try to hold the yarn leading to the ball wound round your little finger and over the tip of the first

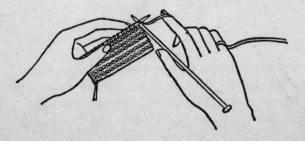

finger of your right hand. Use the tip of your first finger to pass the yarn between the needle points instead of letting go of the needle each time you make a stitch.

The yarn flows more steadily because it is 'anchored' by being round your finger. Never let it be so tight that it is difficult to get the needle into the stitches. Relax! It's fun to knit – don't turn it into hard work.

Now, when you can only work slowly, is the time to master the right way of holding the yarn as well as to learn to make the stitches. Some people are in such a rush that they never learn; with every stitch they knit, they drop the yarn and so have to pick it up again for the next stitch. (If they had stopped and learned it properly right at the start, they would be able to knit far more quickly, and their knitting would be more even.)

How to cast off

So you have now knitted quite a few rows. Next you must learn how to stop.

If you slipped the knitting off the needles, the stitches would be loose and would begin to unravel. Casting off finishes the last row so that the stitches are secured and held in place.

Put the needle with the stitches into your left hand and the empty needle into your right hand.

Knit the first two stitches just as you would for an ordinary row.

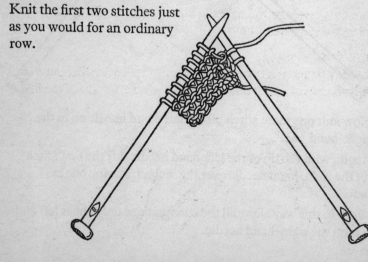

With the tip of the left-hand needle, lift the first stitch you knitted on the right-hand needle over the second stitch

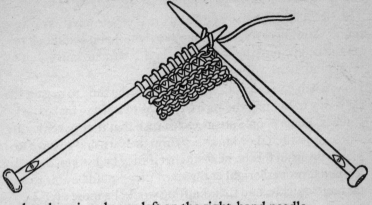

so that there is only one left on the right-hand needle.

Now knit one more stitch off the left-hand needle on to the right-hand one.

Again, with the tip of the left-hand needle, lift the first stitch on the right-hand needle over the second, leaving one as before.

Work in this way along all the stitches until only one is left and it is on the right-hand needle.

Cut the yarn about 10 centimetres from the knitting, and draw the cut end of the yarn through the last stitch and slip it off the needle. Pull the cut end gently to close up the last loop.

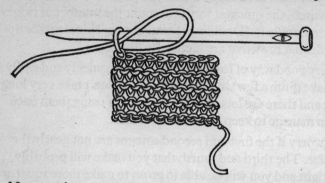

Now you have cast on, knitted and cast off, but a tail of yarn is still hanging from your work. Before you do any more, thread it into a wool needle and darn it into the side or the cast-off edge, on the wrong side where it will not be seen when the work is finished. Always darn in at least 5 cm so that the end is not so short that it will work its way loose. Cut off any yarn that is left over.

Garter stitch

Before you go on to the next section, look at the piece you have knitted. Did you notice what happened as you knitted? As you worked each row, a flat stitch was made facing you, and that stitch had a straight or horizontal loop across it at the back of the work. When you turned the knitting round for the next row, the loop was on the side of the work facing you.

When every row is worked like this, the result is called 'garter stitch'. It looks the same on either side. Garter stitch

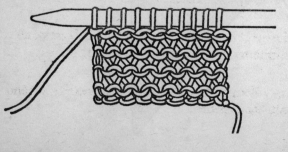

is made up of a flat row and then a ridged row, then another flat row, another ridged row, and so on.

When you want to count how many rows you have worked in garter stitch, the quickest way is to count the number of ridges and then double it. (Doubling the number of ridges makes up for all the flat rows that are hidden by the ridges.)

One very good way of learning to knit more quickly and easily is to make quite a few small squares. They don't take very long to knit and there are lots of different ways of using them once you can manage to keep them the same size.

Don't worry if the first and second squares are not nearly the same size. The third and fourth that you make will probably be all right and you will be able to go on to make more squares that don't vary very much – provided that you always use yarn that is the same thickness.

Patchwork
To make one patch
Using No 8 needles and Patons Double Knitting, cast on 16 stitches. Knit 26 rows, or continue until the length of the work is the same as the width.

Remember that when you measure you should lay the knitting flat. Use your ruler to measure first the width and then the depth of the patch.

Another way of checking that a patch is square is to lay the work flat and fold the cast-on edge over so that it lies along the

side of the knitting, making a triangular shape.
When the side edge is the same length as the cast-on edge, you are ready to cast off.

Cast off and darn in the ends of the yarn.

Here are some patchwork things that you can make with squares.

Small purse

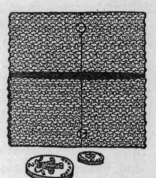

Six squares will make a small purse. Join the squares together into two strips, each three squares long, and then sew the strips together. You now have an oblong two squares wide by three squares deep.

Fold the lower two squares over the middle two and seam the side edges, using a back-stitch seam as shown in Section 11.

Fold the top two squares over as a flap to shut the purse, and fix on a popper or sew on a small square of Velcro fastener. You could even put a small button on top of the popper or Velcro on the right side as an additional finish.

Spectacles case

Six squares will also make a spectacles case. Again, sew the six squares together to form a piece three squares by two squares. Fold in half lengthwise so that there are three squares at the front and three at the back. Seam down the long side and across one of the short edges. This leaves one end open so that the spectacles may be slipped inside.

Patchwork can make a good deal more: a pram or bedcover for

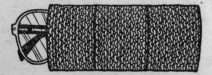

your doll, a cot-cover for a baby, an envelope for keeping your pyjamas in, a cushion for your room.

Here are some other things to make in garter stitch.

Kettle or pot holder

Using No 8 needles and Patons Double Knitting, cast on 32 stitches.

Knit 52 rows, or continue until the length of the work is the same as the width. (You can fold it into a triangle to check this as you did for the patchwork squares.)

Cast off.

Make a second square in exactly the same way. Finish off the ends by darning them in neatly. Place one square on top of the other. Using the wool needle and either the same yarn or a contrasting colour, blanket-stitch all four edges of both squares together. (You will find a diagram showing how to work blanket-stitch in Section 11.)

Hairband

Using No 8 needles and Patons Double Knitting, cast on 10 stitches.

Knit in garter stitch until the strip is *nearly* long enough to reach round your head. (It needs to be about 15 cm too short.)

Cast off.

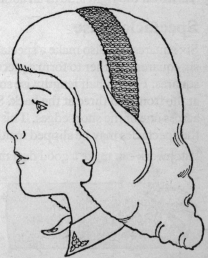

Darn in the ends of the yarn and sew a scrap of elastic 15 cm long on to the strip so that the hairband forms a circle.

The elastic will stretch for you to get the hairband on and then will help to hold it in place.

3 First things first

Now that you can cast on, knit and cast off, the next thing you must try is to *purl* stitches instead of knitting them.

'Knitting' and 'purling' stitches are really the only two ways of working stitches and all designs are built up from these.

Let's try it and see for ourselves.

Purling

Look at the diagrams first and see if you can see the difference between purling and knitting.

Purling is worked in very much the same way, but the needle is put through the stitch *from the back to the front*, instead of from the front to the back as when knitting a stitch.

Put the needle with the stitches you have cast on into your left hand, and take the empty needle in your right hand.

Place the tip of the right-hand needle into the first stitch, from

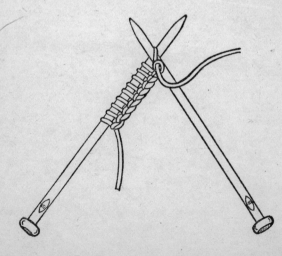

the back towards the front. Have the yarn leading to the ball at the front of the knitting, facing you.

Bring the yarn up and round the tip of the right-hand needle.

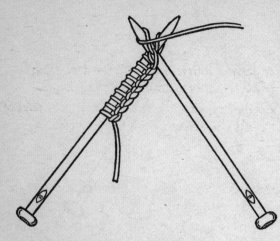

Draw a new loop through the stitch by taking the right-hand needle back with the new loop on it.

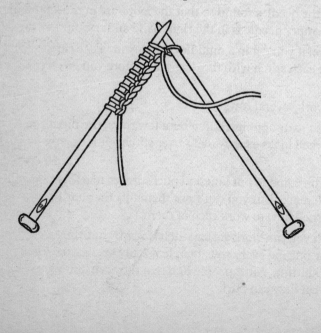

Once the new loop is on the right-hand needle, then you can withdraw the left-hand needle from that stitch completely.

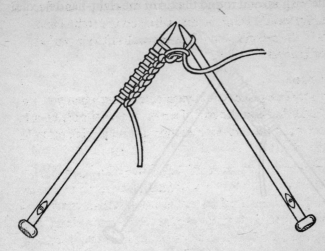

Work all the stitches on the left-hand needle in the same way until all the new loops are on the right-hand needle.

Change the needles round so that the loops are in the left hand and the empty needle is in the right hand and try another row.

As before, if you get in a muddle, start again. Take care to compare each stitch with the diagrams before you go on to the next.

Try to work several rows.

Don't be too disappointed if, after a few rows, the piece you have worked looks exactly like garter stitch – it *is* exactly like it!

(When you come to put knit and purl stitches together you will see a difference. But you can't put them together until you have learned how to work each of them.)

Although you can work garter stitch *either* by knitting every row *or* by purling every row, people usually take garter stitch to mean knitting. Most people find that they can knit more evenly than they can purl.

You can work garter stitch either way – once you've had practice.

To cast off in purl, you follow the same procedure as when you cast off knitwise, slipping the first stitch on the right-hand needle over the second; but of course each stitch is purled instead of knitted.

Joining yarn

There is only one place to join yarn of any sort when you are knitting, and that is at the end of a row. Never simply knot it together or twist the two ends so that you get a thick lump in the middle of a row.

When you have only a short end left, leave it hanging at the side of the work. Take the new ball and, leaving an end long enough to be darned in later (that is, not less than 10 cm), knot the ends *loosely* to prevent the stitches from unravelling. Hold the yarn from the new ball ready to make the first stitch, and work the row knitting or purling in the usual way.

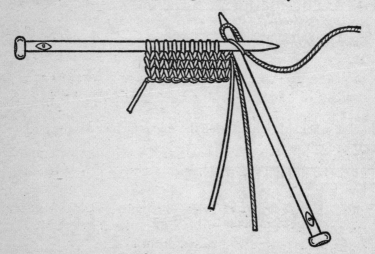

The ends are dealt with later when you come to finish off – the knot is then undone and the ends are darned in.

If you seem to have almost finished a ball, *don't* risk working 'just one more row' before you start a new ball. One row will take four times its length in yarn to knit. If you have less than this, don't start the row. A tail at the end that is not long enough to darn in will simply mean that you 'drop' some of your stitches and spoil your knitting.

Using purl and knit rows for stocking stitch

Using No 8 needles and Patons Double Knitting, cast on 18 stitches.

Knit the first row and then turn the needles and purl the second row.

Work 8 rows more, alternately knitting one row and then turning and purling the next.

Have you done enough to see the difference this makes ?

One side will be smooth, or plain,

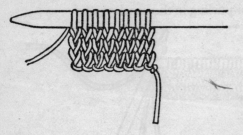

and the other side will have all the ridges on it and is the purl or the rough side.

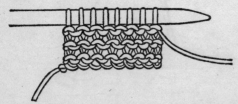

Stocking stitch is the name given when the smooth, plain, knit side is used as the 'right' side, and the rough, purl side is to be the 'wrong' side of whatever you are making.

Sometimes you will find that the purl side is used by the designer as the right side, and when this is so it is called 'reversed stocking stitch'.

Casting off in stocking stitch

Whether you finish with a knit or a purl row, you can cast off quite easily. You already know how to cast off a knit row.

To cast off a purl row, purl the first two stitches and lift the first over the second so that only one stitch remains on the right-hand needle. Purl the next stitch and again

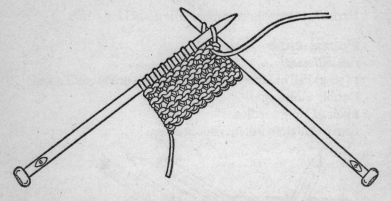

lift the first stitch over the second. Continue until you have cast off all but one stitch. Cut the yarn about 10 cm from the knitting and draw it through the last stitch.

When you have worked a sample and cast it off, you will find that stocking stitch doesn't lie flat on its own, as garter stitch did, but tends to curl round. This is because all the purl stitches are on one side. As you learn more about knitting, you will see how things can be edged so that they are not spoiled by the way stocking stitch curls.

Counting rows

Counting how many rows you have worked in stocking stitch is easiest to do on the wrong side of the knitting. Every ridge is on the wrong, or purl side, so all you have to do is count the number of ridges. There is one ridge for each row worked.

On the right side, the stitches will look like a smaller version of the diagram. You can see how each complete stitch makes a V shape which grows out of the V below it. They don't usually stand out quite as clearly as the ridges, but they are not difficult to count.

Here are some things to make using stocking stitch.

Pencil case

You will need:
1 (50-g) ball of Patons Double Knitting or Patons Trident Double Knitting
1 pair of No 8 needles
1 strip of Velcro fastener about 20 cm long, or 3 large poppers

To work the pencil case
Using No 8 needles and Double Knitting, cast on 48 stitches.

Knit 2 rows.
3rd row Knit.
4th row Purl.
Continue, repeating the 3rd and 4th rows, until your knitting measures 15 cm from the cast-on edge up to the stitches still on the needle. (Did you remember to lay it flat to measure it ?)
Knit 2 rows to finish off.

Cast off and cut the yarn, leaving a 10-cm end to darn in.

To sew up the pencil case
Using the blunt-ended wool needle, darn in the ends neatly. Cut off any tails that are left.

Fold the work in half so that the smooth sides are touching and the cast-on and cast-off edges are together at the top.

Sew the ends of the case using back-stitch. (You will find a diagram showing you how to do this in Section 11.)

Before you turn it right side out, sew one Velcro strip to each edge of the top so that it is level with the edge of the knitting. Sew on the poppers if you prefer to use them.

Turn the case right side out so that the seamed ends are hidden and it is ready for use.

Small pouch

This can be used to hold your purse, handkerchief and shopping list, or you can make it to hold clothes pegs. Slung round your neck on its ribbon or cord, it will leave your hands free to peg out the clothes.

You will need:
1 (50-g) ball of Patons Double Knitting or Patons Trident Double Knitting
1 pair of No 8 needles
about 0.75 metre ribbon or cord for strap
one large popper or a small strip of Velcro fastener

To work the pouch
Using No 8 needles and Double Knitting, cast on 36 stitches.

Knit 4 rows.
5th row Knit.
6th row Purl.

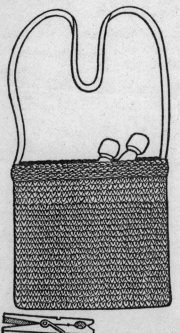

Repeat the 5th and 6th rows until your knitting measures 25 cm when you lay it flat.

Knit 4 rows.

Cast off, and cut the yarn leaving a 10-cm end to darn in.

To sew up the pouch

Darn in the ends and cut off any yarn that is left.

Fold the pouch in half with the smooth sides touching, and, using back-stitch, seam the ends together. (There is a diagram showing how to do back-stitch in Section 11.)

Sew the popper in place, or sew a small piece of Velcro on to each side on the wrong side.

Turn the pouch right side out.

Sew the ribbon or cord neatly just inside the top at either side. Make sure that you sew it securely.

4 Lacy things

Knitting or purling should always be even, without gaps and holes. But sometimes you *want* holes. You need them for buttonholes, and they are very useful if you want to thread ribbon through knitting – either as a decoration, or to tie a neck or make a belt at the waist of a dress. Holes are also needed if you want to knit a lacy pattern.

To make a hole
The best way to understand how a hole is made is to try it out on a small sample.

Using No 8 needles and Double Knitting, cast on 10 stitches. Work 4 rows in stocking stitch. (That means knit 1 row, purl 1 row, knit 1 row and purl 1 more row.)

Next row Knit 4 stitches, put the yarn over the needle from front to back, and then put the tip of the right-hand needle through both the next 2 stitches at the same time

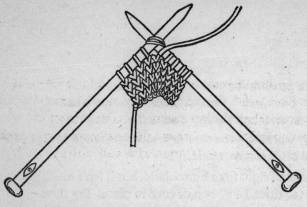

and make a stitch in the usual way. Then knit the last 4 stitches as usual.

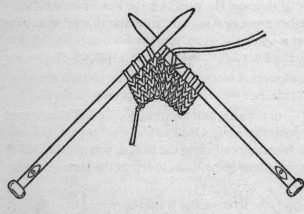

The diagrams show you each step.

Purl 1 row. You should still have 10 stitches. If you have only got 9, it means that you have not purled the yarn that you put over the needle. Try it again.

It took so many words the last time, see if you can follow these shorter instructions. They mean just the same.

Cast on 10 stitches and work 4 rows stocking stitch.

Next row Knit 4 stitches, put the yarn over the needle and knit the next 2 stitches together, knit 4 stitches.

Work 3 rows more in stocking stitch.

Sometimes the order is changed, but it makes no difference to the finished hole.

Would you like to try it in the different order ?

Try it on the sample you have just made.
Next row Knit 4, knit the next 2 stitches together, put the yarn over the needle, knit the last 4 stitches.

Finish by working 3 rows more in stocking stitch so that you can see what you have made.

One hole is all right for a buttonhole, but it isn't much good if you want to thread a ribbon or cord in place. Try this :

Using No 8 needles and Double Knitting, cast on 14 stitches. Knit 1 row. Purl 1 row. Then knit 1 more row and purl 1 row.
Next row * Knit 2, put the yarn over the needle and knit the next 2 stitches together. Go back to the star (*) and work what comes after it again and again until there are only 2 stitches still on the left-hand needle; then knit these 2 stitches.

Work 3 rows more in stocking stitch so that you can see what you have made. Are there still 14 stitches on your needles ?

The star (*), or asterisk, as it is properly called, is always used to mark a point that you go back to and repeat again. Sometimes you repeat from there all along the row, or you may be told in the instructions how many times to repeat the same group of stitches.

Without the *, the instructions would have read like this :

Next row Knit 2, put the yarn over the needle and knit the next 2 stitches together, knit 2, put the yarn over the needle and knit the next 2 stitches together, knit 2, put the yarn over the needle and knit the next 2 stitches together, knit the last 2 stitches.

See how much longer this takes, and also how much more difficult it is to find your place!

If everything was written out like this, there would be very little room left for all the 'things' you are still going to make!

When you start to work from other books, you might find that brackets ( ) are used instead of a star *, but they mean the same. If brackets were used the same instructions would read like this:

Next row (Knit 2, put the yarn over the needle and knit the next 2 stitches together), repeat until 2 stitches are left, knit these 2 stitches.

In this book, however, the asterisk * is always used.

Here are some things to make.

Napkin ring

You will need:

1 (50-g) ball of Patons Double Knitting
1 pair of No 8 needles
1 small button
a small piece of contrasting yarn to
    make the trimming – you will
    need about 60 cm

To work the napkin ring

Using No 8 needles and Double Knitting, cast on 26 stitches.

Knit 4 rows.

5th row Knit.

6th row Knit 2, purl until 2 stitches are left, knit these 2 stitches.

Work the 5th and 6th rows twice more.

Next row Knit 2, * knit 2 together, put the yarn over the needle and knit next 2 stitches, repeat from the * until all the stitches have been worked.

Next row Work in the same way as the 6th row.

Repeat the 5th and 6th rows twice more.

Knit 4 rows. Cast off.

To finish the napkin ring
Darn in the ends and trim off any tails left.

Use the hole nearest the edge as a buttonhole; sew a button at the other end on the edge so that when it is buttoned up it forms a circle.

Using the No 8 needles, cast on 22 stitches with the contrasting yarn. Don't knit any rows, but cast off again. This makes a coloured lace which you can thread through the holes to trim it, and also to show just who the ring belongs to: you can make each member of your family a ring with a different-coloured trim. Sew the ends of the trim on the inside so that it won't slip out!

Doll's pillowcase

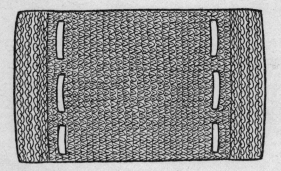

Why not try something really lacy and see how you get on using finer yarn and thinner needles.

You will need:
1 (25-g) ball of Patons Trident 4-ply
1 pair of No 10 needles
50 cm narrow baby ribbon

To work the pillowcase
Using No 10 needles and 4-ply yarn, cast on 26 stitches.
Knit 8 rows.
Work 2 rows stocking stitch – that is, 1 row knit, 1 row purl.

Next row Knit 2, * knit 2 stitches together, put the yarn over the needle and knit the next 2 stitches, repeat from the * to the end of the row.

Purl 1 row.

Go on working in stocking stitch until your work measures 18 cm from the cast-on edge. Finish by working a purl row.

Next row Knit 2, * knit 2 stitches together, put the yarn over the needle and knit the next 2 stitches, repeat from the * to the end of the row.

Purl 1 row.

Knit 4 rows.

Cast off.

Work a second piece for the back of the pillowcase in the same way.

To finish the pillowcase

Place the smooth sides together and seam along the edges using back-stitch, shown in Section 11. You can leave both the garter-stitch ends open, or you can seam one end and leave the other open to take the pillow in and out easily.

Cut the ribbon in half. Thread one piece through the holes at one end and the other piece through those at the other end.

Stitch the ends of each ribbon circle together inside the pillowcase where they won't show.

5 Striping things

One of the easiest ways of making a pattern, even on straight pieces of knitting, is to use more than one colour and knit in stripes.

Changing to use a different colour is just like joining in a new ball of yarn. Always change colours at the start of a row, never in the middle of one.

Working wide stripes

When the stripes are more than 4 or 6 rows deep, it is easiest to cut the yarn you have been using, leaving an end at the side of the work not less than 10 cm long. Then join the new colour in just as if it was a new ball, again leaving a 10-cm tail.

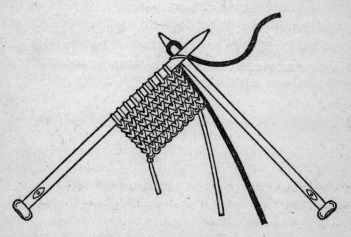

Knot both ends loosely together. (The knot can be undone and the ends darned in when the knitting is finished and you are ready to sew up whatever you are making.)

Continue working with the new colour until you want to change and then do just the same again, never forgetting to leave ends that are long enough for easy darning in.

Working narrow stripes

For narrow stripes that are only 2 or 4 rows deep, you don't need to cut the yarn every time you change colour – it means such a lot of work to darn all the ends in.

When you have worked the first stripe, leave the yarn hanging at the row end and don't cut it off. Join in the next colour as if it was a new ball (leaving a 10-cm end as before). When you have finished your second stripe, leave the yarn hanging – don't cut it off. Pick up the first colour and use it again.

You must watch just one thing: when you take the yarn up to start using it again, you must not pull it so tight that you draw the row ends together. Leave just as much slack as it needs

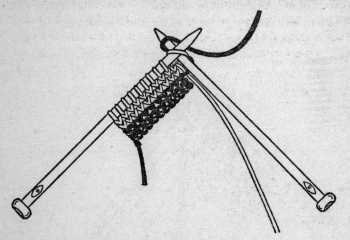

to go from the last stitch you used it for to the first of the next stripe. It isn't any better if you leave a big loop, because the end stitches will work loose.

You can work three colours over narrow stripes if you are careful; but if you have to 'carry' the yarn over more than 4 or 6 rows before using it again, you might do better to cut it.

Odd numbers of rows

You can only take the yarn up the side of the work if you are going to finish using it at the same side as the other colour – that is, if you work an even number of rows. Working only one row means that you will finish away from the side where the other colour is hanging, and so you will need to cut the yarn and rejoin it. If you are making up the pattern of stripes by yourself, then always think about this before you start. It is easiest to make narrow stripes of 2 or 4 rows each.

Joining with a straight line

Whenever you are knitting stripes in garter stitch, you need to watch which side of the work is facing when you start a new colour, or you may find that the stripe has a broken edge instead of starting off with a straight line.

To be sure of a straight line, you must always start a new stripe with a row when the right side of the work is facing you.

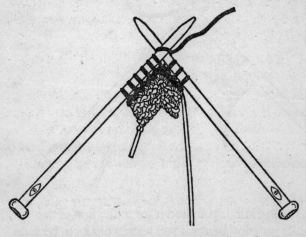

If you then look at what has happened on the wrong side, you will see how the loops make an uneven edge.

(When you have knitted lots of things and are using instructions from other books and magazines, you may find a pattern where the designer has intentionally made use of this broken, loopy edge, but it is better to know what to expect.)

Stripes in reversed stocking stitch are a little more difficult to work unless you are happy to have this broken edge, but when you are more experienced you will understand how to make straight stripes, even in this type of knitting.

Stripes that go up and down your knitting are quite different and are not as easy to make as stripes that go across . . . at least until you have learned a little more.

Mixing yarns

Stripes mean hunting around for different colours. One thing needs watching when you do this. You mustn't get so delighted with the colours that you forget a rule of knitting: stripes *must* be worked in yarns that are of exactly the same thickness. You can't use one thick yarn and one thin yarn and hope that the stripes are going to look even. You must choose two double-knitting yarns, for example, or two 4-ply yarns.

Also under this rule comes the fact that if one yarn is wool, then don't choose nylon to go with it.

You *can* mix some things quite happily. Yarns that are the same thickness can easily be used together even if they are not both smooth. Sometimes you get a yarn that is made with bumps in it, and nubbly stripes alternating with smooth ones look very good, provided the yarns are more or less the same thickness.

Smooth yarn can also look good striped with fluffy yarn, with flecked tweed yarn or with random-dyed yarn.

You can mix types of yarn that are made from the same thing and are of approximately the same thickness. It's a good idea to check that they all need the same washing treatment, too; there is not much point in using something that needs a very cool wash (or even likes to be dry-cleaned) along with a yarn that needs a warm wash.

This still leaves plenty of choice, and there are many different ways in which stripes can be most unusual and, nearly always, very fashionable.

Here is something striped to make.

Striped work bag

What about a neat bag for keeping your work in ? It's time that you made your own.

You will need:
4 (50-g) balls of different-coloured Patons Double Plus
1 pair of No 8 needles

How to knit the work bag
Using No 8 needles and the 1st colour, cast on 60 stitches.
Starting with a knit row, work 10 rows in stocking stitch. (That means you knit 1 row and purl 1 row. Then you repeat these 2 rows 4 times more.)

Cut the yarn, leaving a 10-cm length for darning in. Now get the 2nd colour ready.

Work 10 rows using the 2nd colour. Cut the end and join in the 3rd colour.

Work 10 rows using the 3rd colour. Cut the end and join in the 4th colour.

Work 10 rows using the 4th colour. Cut the end.
Now work 10 rows more in each of the 1st, 2nd and 3rd colours.
Join the 4th colour in again. Work 4 rows.
You are going to make a row of holes in the next row, so that
you can pull the bag shut with a draw-string.

Eyelet-hole row With 4th colour, knit 1, yarn over needle, knit
2 together, * knit 6, yarn over needle, knit 2 together, repeat
from the * until only 1 stitch is still on the left-hand needle.
Knit this stitch.

Now knit 9 rows, so that you make a garter-stitch edge that
won't curl over. Cast off.

Work a second piece in exactly the same way.

To make up the work bag
Place both pieces together with the smooth sides touching.
Using back-stitch (see Section 11), join the sides and the cast-on
edges.

Turn the bag right side out.

Cut 2 strands of each colour yarn 60 cm long.

Take 1 piece of each colour and, starting at one side, thread
them through the holes at the top of your bag. When all 4
strands have been threaded through the eyelet holes, knot the
ends at the side so that they form a circle and can't come out.

Take the remaining 4 threads and put them through the eyelet
holes in the same way, but starting from the opposite side of the
bag. Knot them at the other side, making a 'handle' at either
side.

6 Shaping things

Learning to shape things is very important, not because it is difficult in any way, but because you will then be able to make anything that you like.

There are two very different ways of making any piece of knitting larger and two ways of making it smaller.

One way is to increase or decrease, and gives a gradual shaping; the other is to add or take away several stitches at once and means that the edge will have a piece that juts in or out suddenly.

To make knitting larger suddenly
To do this, you simply cast on extra stitches at the beginning of the row. If you cast on only one stitch, then the edge will only take a small step out; if you cast on a lot of stitches, it will jut out quite a lot and will form a sharp corner.

Although you will already have knitted several rows, the method of casting on additional stitches is exactly the same as when you cast on at the start of knitting.

The tip of the right-hand needle is put between the first two stitches on the needle in your left hand, and a new loop is drawn through and placed on to the left-hand needle.

When you want to cast on more than one stitch, you put the needle back between the two stitches that are now on the end of the left-hand needle and make another stitch; continue like this until you have cast on as many as you need.

You do need to remember one thing: you can only cast on at the beginning of a row. So, if you want to cast on at both sides, you must work the right-hand edge first, then knit across to the other side; when you turn the work at the end of this row, that edge then becomes the right-hand one and can have its stitches cast on.

To make knitting smaller suddenly

Casting off works in the same way. Unless you break the yarn and rejoin it, you can only cast off at the beginning of a row. If you want to cast off stitches at both sides, then you must cast off the stitches at one side first, work across the row, turn, and then cast off the second side.

The method is exactly the same as for ordinary casting off, except that you stop when you have lifted over as many stitches as you want to 'lose'.

When that number is cast off, then you are ready to work the rest of the row in the normal way.

To shape gradually

To make a piece of knitting larger is called to 'increase' it and you need to work 'increases' to do this. When you make it smaller, you 'decrease' it and work what are called 'decreases'.

There are many different ways of doing both, but there is no need to learn them all now. In this book we shall only use one type of increase and two types of decrease.

Sometimes increases are worked in the middle of the row, but usually they are right at the edge. Because a tidy edge means that sewing up is easier, I always plan to have edge increases *inside* the edge stitches so that the edge doesn't become crooked.

Increasing one stitch

The method used in this book is the neatest method and can be used anywhere in the row, just wherever it is needed.

Try it and see how easy it is to make shapes.

Using No 8 needles and double-knitting yarn, cast on 10 stitches.

Knit 1 row and purl 1 row.
3rd row Knit 2 stitches. Using the tip of the right-hand needle, lift the thread before the next stitch. Place it on the

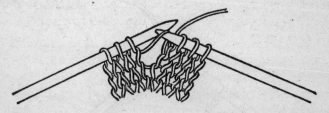

left-hand needle when you have lifted it, and then turn it once so that it is twisted to form a loop. Can you see how this is done in the diagrams?

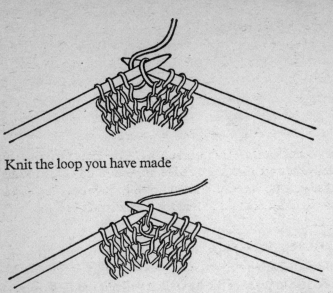

Knit the loop you have made

and then knit all the stitches until only 2 are left. 'Make' another stitch by using the right-hand needle to lift the thread before the next stitch, turn it and, once it is on the left-hand needle, knit it and the last 2 stitches as well.

Are there 12 stitches on the needle now?

Purl 1 row.

Whenever you need to increase a stitch, the words 'Make 1' will mean that you lift the next thread, twist it and knit it in this way. Try it again.

Next row Knit 2, make 1, knit 8, make 1, knit 2.
Purl 1 row. Now there should be 14 stitches.
Next row Knit 2, make 1, knit 10, make 1, knit 2.
Purl 1 row. Now have you got 16 stitches?

Before you take this sample off the needles, see if you can decrease too.

Decreasing one stitch (1)
You have already done this, so it can't be difficult!

When you made a hole, you knitted two stitches together – and knitting two stitches together is the simplest way of decreasing.

53

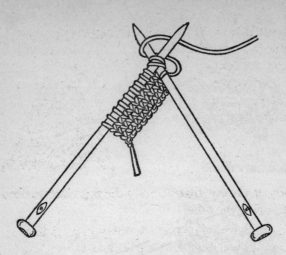

When you made a hole, you didn't get one stitch less in the row because in place of the lost stitch you put the yarn over the needle to make a new loop. When you are decreasing, you don't do that.

The two stitches knitted together complete the decrease.

Try it on the increase sample you have just made.

Next row Knit 1, knit 2 stitches together, knit the next 10 stitches, knit 2 stitches together, knit 1.
Purl 1 row. You should have 14 stitches.
Next row Knit 1, knit 2 stitches together, knit 8, knit 2 stitches together, knit 1.
Purl 1 row.

And now there are 12 stitches. If not, then you had better start again and look at the diagram carefully first!

Can you see that both decreases tend to lie sloping just a little towards the right?

It is because of this that we need to learn one more way of doing a decrease.

Why?

Look at knitted mittens, a baby's bootee or a hand-knitted sweater with raglan sleeves. You will see that when decreases are worked at each side of the piece of knitting, the decreases both slope towards the middle.

The decrease on the right is made to slope towards the middle, or the left, and the decrease on the left side slopes towards the right.

You can already do the one that slopes to the right but we need to find a way of doing the other.

Like everything in knitting, it is very simple and you could really work it out for yourself – but it takes a lot of words to explain it!

Decreasing one stitch (2)

Have you still got 12 stitches ready on the needles?

If not, start again and cast on 12 stitches.

Knit 1 row and purl 1 row.

Next row Knit 1. Using the right-hand needle tip, slip the next stitch over on to the right-hand needle without knitting it at all. Knit the stitch that was beyond it. Then, with the

left-hand needle tip, lift the slipped stitch right over the top of the last stitch you knitted, just as when you cast off a stitch.

Knit the next 6 stitches, knit 2 stitches together, knit the last stitch.

Purl 1 row, and you should have 10 stitches.

The stitch that you decreased at the beginning of the row is shortened to: 'slip 1, knit 1, pass slipped stitch over'. Can you do it again?

Next row Knit 1, slip 1, knit 1, pass slipped stitch over, knit 4, knit 2 stitches together, knit 1.

Purl 1 row. You should now have 8 stitches, and should be able to see the way the stitches are sloping – both sets of decreases towards the centre of the work.

Did you wonder what to do with the yarn leading to the ball when you slipped the stitch?

You simply leave it at the back of the work (that is, the side away from you, behind the knitting), while you slip the stitch, and then pick it up and go on knitting as if you had never let go of it.

It is very useful to know how to decrease two stitches at once, especially if you are working to a point.

Decreasing two stitches in one place
To decrease two stitches at once, you put together two things that you have already learned: slipping a stitch and knitting two stitches together. Put together, they make a tidy way of getting rid of two stitches.

If you had 10 stitches on the needle and wanted to get rid of 2 in the centre, you would knit 3 stitches, slip the next stitch, knit the following 2 stitches together

and then, using the tip of the left-hand needle, lift the slipped stitch over the 2 that have been knitted together.

Finally, knit the last 4 stitches. And that really is all you need to know about how to make shapes.

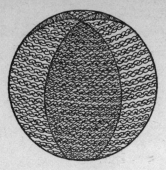

Coloured ball

A ball is a good thing to make to practise shaping.
This ball is made in six sections that are sewn together after
they have been knitted. This time the instructions have been
given for one colour only, but if you enjoy knitting the ball,
why not see how many different combinations of colours you
can think of? You could make three sections in one colour and
three in another, as above, or you could make all six in different
colours. You could knit it in wide or narrow stripes, or you
could knit a broad band through the centre of each section.
Can you think of any other designs?

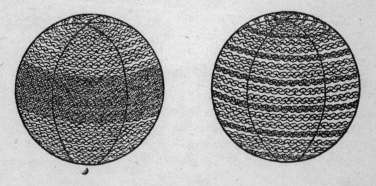

You will need (for a ball in one colour):
1 (50-g) ball of Patons Double Knitting
1 pair of No 8 needles
kapok, foam or clean chopped-up nylons or tights for stuffing

58

To work the ball

Using No 8 needles and Double Knitting, cast on 3 stitches. The ball is worked entirely in garter stitch.

Knit 2 rows.

3rd row Knit 1, make 1, knit 1, make 1, knit 1.

Knit 3 rows.

7th row Knit 1, make 1, knit 3, make 1, knit 1.

Knit 3 rows.

11th row Knit 1, make 1, knit 5, make 1, knit 1.

Knit 3 rows.

15th row Knit 1, make 1, knit 7, make 1, knit 1.

Knit 3 rows.

19th row Knit 1, make 1, knit 9, make 1, knit 1.

Knit 7 rows.

27th row Knit 1, knit 2 together, knit 7, knit 2 together, knit 1.

Knit 3 rows.

31st row Knit 1, knit 2 together, knit 5, knit 2 together, knit 1.

Knit 3 rows.

35th row Knit 1, knit 2 together, knit 3, knit 2 together, knit 1.

Knit 3 rows.

39th row Knit 1, knit 2 together, knit 1, knit 2 together, knit 1.

Knit 3 rows.

43rd row Knit 1, slip 1 stitch, knit 2 together, lift slipped stitch over the other 2, knit 1.

Knit 1 row. Cast off.

Knit 5 other sections in exactly the same way.

To sew the ball together

Join each section to the next from top to bottom using backstitch (see Section 11). When you have completed five seams, form them into a ball and work half of the sixth seam. Stuff the ball and then finish the seam neatly using ladder stitch (see Section 11).

7 Ribbing things

You have already put knit stitches and purl stitches together in rows and seen how they made stocking stitch instead of the garter stitch that you got when you worked all knit rows or all purl rows.

When you made stocking stitch, you put one complete row of knitted stitches after one complete row of purled stitches.

Now let's see what happens if you mix knit and purl stitches in the same row, and then work the next row with knit on top of purl, and purl on top of knit.

When you make upright or vertical rows like this it is called 'ribbing'. There are lots of different types of ribbing, but one of the simplest and most often used is the one we shall try first.

Ribbing is a tremendously useful edging for many things. It is particularly good in wool, which is very elastic. Knitted on the edge of a sleeve, ribbing lets your hand through easily, but springs back into place to keep the wind out and sit neatly round your wrist. Ribbing is slightly less elastic in nylon and certain man-made fibres, and not very elastic in cotton, but it still has its uses.

When ribbing is arranged like this first sample it is called 'two-and-two ribbing'.

To work two-and-two ribbing
Using No 8 needles and double-knitting yarn, cast on 12 stitches.

1st row *Knit 2 stitches, take the yarn forward so that you can purl the next 2 stitches,

purl these and then take the yarn back
so that you are ready to knit again.

Repeat from the * along the row until you have worked
all the stitches.

Count the stitches. If there are more than 12, you have
probably put the yarn *over* the needle and made a loop when
changing from knit to purl or from purl to knit.

Try another row in the same way, making certain that you
always get the yarn into the right position for the type of stitch
you are going to work next – yarn forward for purl, back for
knit.

Work several rows more until you can see the line that the
stitches are making.

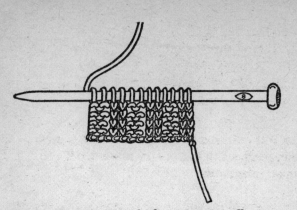

Work at least 10 rows before you cast off.

You can cast off in rib quite easily.

To cast off in rib
Knit the first two stitches, then lift the first one over the second, off the right-hand needle. Bring the yarn forward, then purl the next stitch and lift one stitch off the right-hand needle. Purl the next stitch, too, and lift it off. Two knit stitches will come next, so take the yarn back to knit the next stitch before lifting one over and off the right-hand needle. When you come to the last stitch, cut the yarn leaving a 10-cm tail and draw this through the last loop in the usual way.

Do you see what you do ? You work the stitch exactly as you would if you'd been going to work a whole row, but each time you get two stitches on the right-hand needle, you lift one over the other and off the needle.

You can always cast off without spoiling the pattern by working in this way.

Now that the sample is off the needles, do you see how it springs back into place when you pull it sideways ?

To work one-and-one ribbing
Using No 8 needles and double-knitting yarn, cast on 14 stitches.

1st row *Knit 1, take the yarn forward, purl 1, take the yarn back, repeat from the * until all the stitches have been worked.

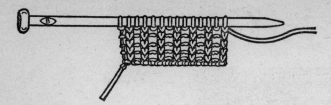

Repeat the first row until you have worked at least 10 rows. Cast off, working each stitch as it would be worked if you had worked a normal ribbed row.

Ribs can be made as wide as you like: you can have three knit and three purl stitches, or even four stitches of each kind.

The wider the rib is, the less elastic it becomes.

Both the ribs you worked had an equal number of knit and of purl stitches.

Work a sample of one-and-four rib.

To work one-and-four ribbing

Using No 8 needles and double-knitting yarn, cast on 20 stitches.

1st row *Knit 4, purl 1, repeat from the * to the end of the row.
2nd row *Knit 1, purl 4, repeat from the * to the end of the row.
Repeat the first and second rows until you have worked at least 10 rows, then cast off.

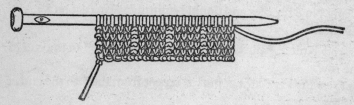

One-and-four rib, knit side

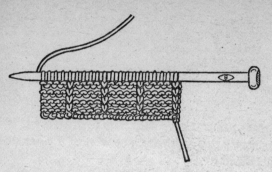

One-and-four rib, purl side

Can you see how in your sample the wide rib (which is a panel of stocking stitch) begins to curl at the edge and doesn't lie as neatly as two-and-two or one-and-one rib?

Wide ribs look very nice as the centre of a rug or when they are edged with a narrow rib, but they do not have as much of the elastic quality as the narrower, evenly spaced ribs.

Practise your ribbing by making this cap.

Ribbed cap

You will need:
1 (50-g) ball of Patons Double Knitting or Patons Trident Double Knitting
1 pair of No 8 needles

To work the cap
Using No 8 needles and double-knitting yarn, cast on 86 stitches.

1st row Knit 2, * purl 2, knit 2, repeat from the * to the end of the row.
2nd row Purl 2, * knit 2, purl 2, repeat from the * to the end of the row.
Repeat the 1st and 2nd rows until the work measures 10 cm from the cast-on edge.

To shape the top
1st row Knit 2 together, * purl 2, knit 2 together, repeat from the * to the end.

2nd row Purl 1, * knit 2, purl 1, repeat from the * to the end.

3rd row Knit 1, * purl 2, knit 1, repeat from the * to the end.

4th row Purl 1, * knit 2, purl 1, repeat from the * to the end.

5th row Knit 1, * purl 2, knit 1, repeat from the * to the end.

6th row Purl 1, * knit 2 together, purl 1, repeat from the * to the end.

7th row Knit 1, * purl 1, knit 1, repeat from the * to the end.

8th row Purl 1, * knit 1, purl 1, repeat from the * to the end.

9th row Knit 1, purl 1, * slip 1, knit 2 together, pass the slipped stitch over, purl 1, repeat from the * to the last stitch, knit 1.

10th row *Purl 1, knit 1, repeat from the * to the last stitch, purl 1.

Last row Knit 1, * knit 2 together, repeat from the * to the end.

Cut an end about 30 cm long. Thread this end through the wool needle, and then pass it through all the loops left on the knitting needle.

Draw the stitches up together and use the same end to sew up the seam from the top to the cast-on edge. Sew it on the right side using ladder stitch, or on the wrong side using back-stitch (see Section 11).

Sew a pompon or two tassels to the top centre – Section 11 tells you how to make these.

8 Patterns on things

You have tried stocking stitch, which is a row of knit then a row of purl stitches, and you have seen what happens when you put ribs of knit and purl stitches above each other in groups. What do you think happens when you start mixing up the loops of the purl stitches and the smooth Vs of the knitted stitches?

They can be used in many other ways to build up designs, from very simple spot patterns to much more complicated-looking patterns. They really only *look* more complicated, for, although it may mean reading more instructions, knitting and purling stitches in any order is easy – as you have found out for yourself.

Moss stitch starts just like one-and-one rib, but because a knit stitch is put over a knit stitch and a purl stitch over a purl stitch (instead of a knit over a purl and a purl over a knit) the result is very different, and nothing like rib at all.

To work moss stitch
Using No 8 needles and double-knitting yarn, cast on 11 stitches.

1st row Knit 1, * purl 1, knit 1, repeat from the * to the end of the row.

Repeat this row 9 times more.

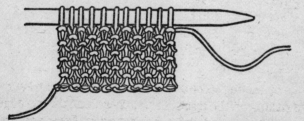

Because the stitches are not in lines, and because there are as many Vs as purled loops, the knitting doesn't curl – it lies flat and so makes a very good border.

Grouping the stitches together in a different way gives us another stitch that lies flat and is attractive too. It is called basket stitch and looks like basket-weave.

To work basket stitch
Using No 8 needles and double-knitting yarn, cast on 12 stitches.

1st row *Purl 3, knit 3, repeat from the * to the end of the row. Work the 1st row 3 times more.
5th row *Knit 3, purl 3, repeat from the * to the end of the row. Work the 5th row 3 times more.

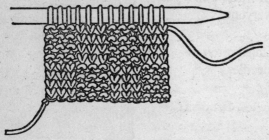

Now go back to the 1st row and work all eight rows once again. Can you see the squared pattern taking shape?

As you begin to make more things, you will realize how many different ways knit and purl stitches can be grouped, and what exciting patterns can be made.

Knitting stitches in groups
Sometimes you will want to knit only some of the stitches on a needle. If you make the hot-water-bottle cover at the end of this section, you will have to knit each of the straps after the other stitches are cast off.

This is done by leaving some of the stitches on the right-hand needle and casting off the rest of the stitches along the top edge until you come to the stitches for the next strap. After working these, you turn the knitting and work the rest of this strap first;

when you have finished it, you cast off, and then the yarn is rejoined to the stitches that have been left unworked on the needle.

To rejoin yarn
Join it into the first stitch leaving a 10-cm end, just as if it was a new ball of yarn, and continue with what the instructions tell you to do next. The end can be darned in after.

Here are some things to make to practise the patterns you've just learned.

Washing-up cloth

Nothing could be easier to knit, and think how it will show off your cleverness to everyone!

You will need:
1 hank of dishcloth cotton
1 pair of No 7 needles

To work the cloth
Using No 7 needles, cast on 21 stitches.

1st row Knit 1, * purl 1, knit 1, repeat from the * to the end.
Repeat the 1st row until the work is square. (Remember to lay it flat when you measure it.)
Cast off.

To finish the cloth

Darn in the ends.
To make it ready for hanging, make a small loop in one corner with 3 strands of cotton, and then work blanket-stitch neatly and closely round the loop. (You can see how to work blanket-stitch in Section 11.)

Hot-water-bottle cover

You will need:

2 (50-g) balls of Patons Double
   Knitting or Patons Trident
   Double Knitting
1 pair of No 8 needles
2 small buttons

To work the cover

Front

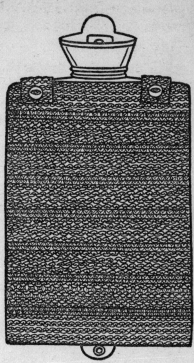

Using No 8 needles, cast on
50 stitches.
Knit 9 rows.
10th row Purl.
Repeat these 10 rows until the
work measures 25 cm,
ending with a 10th row.
Knit 8 rows more. Cast off.

Back

Using No 8 needles, work just
as for the front until the last 8
rows have been worked, but
don't cast off.

To work the straps

Next row Cast off 4 stitches, knit 9 stitches, cast off the centre
24 stitches, knit to the end of the row.
Next row Cast off 4 stitches, knit 9 stitches, and turn to work
the strap on these 9 stitches. (Leave the other 9 stitches at the
other side on the same needle, on a spare needle or on a
stitch-holder as you prefer.)
Knit 8 rows.
Next row Knit 3, knit 2 together, put yarn over needle, knit 4.
Knit 4 rows more. Cast off.
With the wrong side of the work facing you, rejoin the yarn to

the first stitch of the 9 for the other strap (leaving an end to darn in), and knit 9 rows.

Next row Knit 3, knit 2 together, put yarn over needle, knit 4. Knit 4 rows more. Cast off.

To make up the cover

Place the right sides together and with back-stitch (see Section 11) seam up the sides and along the bottom edge, leaving a gap in the centre of 6 cm for the hanger of your bottle to come through. Turn right side out and sew buttons on the top front edge in line with the buttonholes.

9 Colourful things

Stripes are a way of combining colours, but they only use one colour in a row. It's fun to be able to knit more than one colour in the same row.

Patterns using a number of colours are very often worked in stocking stitch, because the smooth texture of the finished knitting lets the pattern show up clearly.

It is also best to keep designs small, because the colour that is not being used has to be taken across the back of the colour that is in use. If you try to carry it across too many stitches, you are more likely to make it too tight. Puckered work won't look very nice when you have finished.

Sometimes instructions for this type of knitting are written in words and a different letter stands for each of the colours that are used; other times a chart is given which shows each stitch and the colour it is to be knitted in. The chart is usually worked out on squared paper and has beside it a list of which colours the different signs represent.

The best thing is to try a sample. When you have tried both methods for the same pattern, you will understand how they work, and will be able to set about using whichever method you meet in patterns in future.

Colourful patterns by chart

On the chart overleaf each square represents a stitch. The background colour is shown by the empty squares and is called A. B shows where the first contrast is used, and C shows where the second contrast is used. You can choose your own colours for A, B and C, although the designer may suggest a colour scheme, perhaps making A stand for cream, B for brown and C for green.

In some knitting patterns the different colours are shown in the chart by symbols instead of letters – a cross for the first contrast and a dot for the second contrast, for example.

The rows are numbered with the odd rows (knit rows) on the right and the even rows (purl rows) on the left. The first row would usually be a knit row and the first square on the right would show which colour to start with. You would then work along the row to the end, working repeats if they are marked, as the whole chart will probably be too large to print. At the end of the row (when you turn the needles to start the next row) you cannot turn the chart, so the purl row is read from left to right instead, beginning with the box or square on the far left and working along to the last square on the right.

Although the chart diagram here shows three repeats, most printed patterns usually give only one and it may be marked

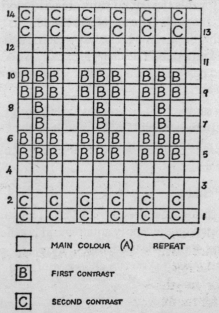

(as the diagram is) with brackets to show where it starts and finishes.

The method of knitting and purling the stitches is exactly the same as normal. The only difference comes when you stop one colour and start another: it is just a case of leaving one colour hanging behind the work, picking up the other colour and working with this until you leave it and return to the first. When you take a colour across some worked stitches to use it again, *don't* pull it tight and *don't* leave a slack loop. It needs to be just the width of the knitting when it is smoothed out – just as firm as when you carry the yarn up the side of a stripe, before using it again.

The yarn is always carried across the stitches on the purl side of the work, which is the wrong side when the knitting is finished.

The same pattern in words

In words it takes up much more room to explain than on the chart! Written out in full, the same pattern would read:

1st row *Knit 1 with A, knit 1 with C, repeat from the * to the end of the row.

2nd row *Purl 1 with C, purl 1 with A, repeat from the * to the end of the row.

3rd row Using A, knit.

4th row Using A, purl.

5th row *Knit 1 with A, knit 3 with B, repeat from the * to the end of the row.

6th row *Purl 3 with B, purl 1 with A, repeat from the * to the end of the row.

7th row *Knit 2 with A, knit 1 with B, knit 1 with A, repeat from the * to the end of the row.

8th row *Purl 1 with A, purl 1 with B, purl 2 with A, repeat from the * to the end of the row.

9th row Work as given for the 5th row.

10th row Work as given for the 6th row.

11th row Work as given for the 3rd row.
12th row Work as given for the 4th row.
13th row Work as given for the 1st row.
14th row Work as given for the 2nd row.

It is not very difficult to make up your own border or design for a pocket on squared paper. Try your own initials if you can't think what to start with.

Do you remember trying basket stitch? Each square of the pattern was 3 stitches wide but was 4 rows deep. Because knitted stitches are seldom as tall as they are wide, your design will not look quite like the one you have on squared paper; it will be a little taller and skinnier, so allow for this.

Easier colourful patterns

Another way of using two colours on the same row is in fact not quite what it seems. The pattern *looks* as if you have used two colours, but in fact you have used only one. This is done by slipping certain of the stitches on a row while you are using a different colour. Imagine you have been knitting with red and change to white for the next row. If you slip every other stitch, when you get to the end of the row you will have both white and red stitches on the needles. Use red again for the next row,

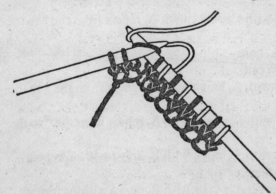

and the work will look as if you had used two colours on the red and white row. It is much easier to work a pattern like this than to use two colours at the same time.

Do you remember keeping the yarn behind the stitch you slipped when we were trying out one of the methods of decreasing? In this type of two-colour pattern (and sometimes you find three- and four-colour patterns that are just as easy) you would always be told whether to slip the stitch keeping the yarn *behind*, or whether the actual strand of yarn across the *front* of the stitch is part of the pattern.

The best way to see is to try these egg cosies yourself.

Egg cosy

This is so attractive when it is finished that you may like to make a tea cosy to match – there are instructions for one in the last section, 'Things galore'.

You will need:
1 (50-g) ball of Patons Double Knitting or Patons Trident Double Knitting in the main shade (A)
1 (50-g) ball of the same type of yarn in a contrast (B)
1 pair of No 8 needles and 1 pair of No 9 needles

To work the egg cosy
Using No 9 needles and A, cast on 33 stitches.
Make a garter-stitch border by knitting 4 rows.
Using No 8 needles, begin the two-colour pattern:
1st row Using A, knit.
2nd row (This is the right side.) Using B, knit 1, * slip 1 with the yarn behind the work, knit 1, repeat from the * to the end of the row.
3rd row Using B, purl 1, * slip 1 keeping the yarn on this side, purl 1, repeat from the * to the end of the row.
4th row Using A, knit.
Work from the 1st to the 4th row 3 times more.
This is the end of the pattern. Cut off the contrast colour, leaving a 10-cm tail to darn in.

Change to No 9 needles and finish the top using A only and working in garter stitch.

Knit 1 row.

Next row Knit 3, * knit 2 together, knit 3, repeat from the * to the end of the row. (27 stitches)

Knit 3 rows.

Next row Knit 3, * knit 2 together, knit 2, repeat from the * to the end of the row. (21 stitches)

Knit 1 row.

Last row Knit 1, * knit 2 together, repeat from the * to the end of the row.

Do *not* cast off, but cut a 15-cm tail and thread it into a wool needle. Thread the needle through all the stitches and slide the knitting needle out. Draw the stitches up and finish off the yarn.

To finish the egg cosy
Seam it on the wrong side from the cast-off edge to the tip using back-stitch (see Section 11).

10 Abbreviating things

You have already seen how much space can be taken up with saying every single word about what you want to knit. It is much easier to learn the sort of 'shorthand' or 'code' used by knitters to make more room for instructions and also to make them far easier to read quickly.

It is time now to look at some of the ways words can be shortened or abbreviated.

You will find as you read printed patterns that 'K' stands for knit just as easily as the whole word, and that 'P' is just as good for purl.

'Stitch' and 'inch' cut down to 'st' and 'in' ('sts' and 'ins' in the plural). 'Cm' is used for centimetre whether you are referring to one or more than one.

'Make 1' is the way we wrote the increase that you have learned, and it can easily be shortened to 'M1'. (In other instructions it might be shortened to 'inc' for increase, while 'dec' is used for decrease.)

All three of the ways you have learned to decrease can be shortened. 'Knit 2 stitches together' can very easily become 'K2 tog'. 'Slip 1 stitch, knit 1 stitch and pass the slipped stitch over' cuts right down to 'sl1, K1, psso', and the other, where you decrease two stitches, becomes 'sl1, K2 tog, psso'.

And that really cuts down on space!

Reading instructions

In instructions, the materials you will need to make the design are usually written first so that you can get everything ready.

The measurements of the finished 'thing' are also given.
These measurements are what the designer got when the 'thing'

was made before it was written out for you. If your work is going to be as nice as the designer's, then these are the measurements that you also should get.

However, not all people knit alike – and yet the way they knit is 'right' for them. So one other guide is given right at the beginning, and you will not be a very clever knit-wit if you fail to make use of it! It is called 'tension'.

Tension

This tells you exactly how many stitches and rows the designer worked to a certain measurement. What the measurement is, whether it is one inch, four inches or 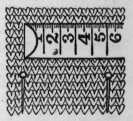 ten centimetres doesn't matter. What *does* matter is that when you try out the knitting with the right yarn and the right needles you should have *the same number of stitches to the same measurement*.

The size of needle that is given is the size the designer used. If you find that you have fewer stitches than she had over the given measurement, then try again using one size smaller needle. If you have too many stitches, try using one size larger. The size of needle is *not* important, but it *is* important to get the same number of stitches as the designer – even if you use chopsticks to do so!

You can't expect your 'thing' to turn out right if you go gaily on ignoring the tension instructions when they have been put there to help you.

One more word about measuring tension.

When you are told that you should knit a certain number of stitches to so many centimetres, don't try to knit just that number and then measure the work. If you are wrong it will never show up on such a small scrap. Always try the tension out over *at least* 10 cm of work.

Always read through instructions *before* you begin to knit. It is most annoying when you already have stitches in mid-air to find that there is an abbreviation that you don't understand, and to have to work out what to do next.

When you want to alter the length of something you are going to knit, remember that you will also change the quantity of yarn that you will need. This can be serious if you make something longer and find that the shop has sold out of that colour. Think about this first.

Where instructions mention a specific yarn, it is always better to try to get that sort rather than to change to another type. If you do change, then you must check the tension very carefully, for it may not work out to the same measurements.

Abbreviations

Here is a list of the abbreviations used in this book:

knit	K
purl	P
stitch(es)	st(s)
metre(s)	m
centimetre(s)	cm
millimetre(s)	mm
gramme(s)	g
knit 2 stitches together	K2 tog
make 1 by lifting the thread before the next stitch	M1
slip 1, knit 1 and pass the slipped stitch over	sl1, K1, psso
slip 1, knit 2 together and pass the slipped stitch over	sl1, K2 tog, psso
put the yarn over the needle	yon
put the yarn round the needle	yrn
with yarn at the back	yb
with yarn at the front	yf
continue	cont
pattern	patt
beginning	beg
stocking stitch	St st
alternate	alt
repeat	rep
remain	rem

11 Sewing things up

Learning to knit things for yourself, your home and your friends is only worth-while if you take the trouble to finish them off and learn to do it well.

It isn't difficult to learn how to do it – but, as with everything, there is a right and a wrong way, and the right way happens to be the easiest.

Darning in ends

The first job is to darn in all the ends. Even this can spoil what you are making if you darn them in carelessly or in the wrong place. When there is to be a seam, see that ends can become part of it – don't go and darn them right into the centre of the wrong side if they can be hidden by the seam. Use small stitches and see that there is enough of the end darned in so that it won't pop out again and perhaps drop stitches.

Pressing knitting

Some things are certainly better for being pressed before you sew them together. Ribbing or garter stitch can be left alone, but stocking stitch is nearly always better pressed.

Before you press *anything*, read the band on the ball. Nowadays pressing instructions are usually marked and you should do what the label tells you. No-iron yarns should *not* be ironed.

Wool can always be pressed (carefully), and many other yarns such as terylene are better for it, but *check first*. It is too late when your knitting has melted!

Fold a blanket on the ironing surface and cover this with a clean cotton cloth. Lay whatever you are going to press, with the wrong side up, on this surface. Hold it in place with pins right on the edge dug into the blanket to keep them from moving. The diagram will show you. The pins need to be close together and the piece of knitting wants to be even, with all the stitches running straight up and down the knitting as well as across it. Work that is pressed to a good shape is very much easier to sew together.

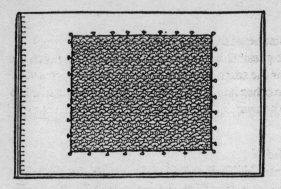

Wring out a clean cotton cloth in warm water and lay it on top of the knitting so that it is covered. Now place the iron on the cloth – but *don't* press, and *don't* slide the iron around as if you are ironing normally. All that is needed is for the heat to make the damp cloth steam – the steam, *not* the iron, will straighten the stitches out and make them even. If you press hard, you will flatten all the stitches you have taken so much care to knit.

Once you have made the cloth dry all over the knitting, by lifting (not pushing) the iron around, you can lift the cloth off. When the knitting is quite dry, take out the pins.

Seaming knitting

Always use a blunt-ended needle for seaming. When you are knitting with very thick yarn, it may be too thick for the needle and for sewing easily. In such a case try to match it with a thinner yarn of the same type.

Back-stitch

Most seams can be worked on the wrong side if you use a back-stitch seam.

Look carefully at the diagram and see how this is done.

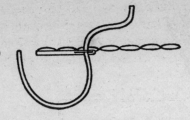

The stitches must be small and they must, of course, be even.
It should not be possible to pull them apart so that you can see
them and so that the seam can be pulled open when you are
finished. On the other hand, the stitches must not be pulled so
very tight that the seam is dragged smaller than the knitting
around it.

Invisible seaming

When you are joining two pieces of knitting in stocking stitch
and the seam is up and down the knitting the same way as the
stitches – like the sides of a jersey or cardigan – then you can
actually put them together so that the seam can't be seen at all,
at least on the right side.

It is called 'mattress stitch seam' or, sometimes, 'ladder stitch'.
Ladder stitch seems far better, because it is just like making
the rungs of a ladder, back and forth from one side of the seam
to the other.

Mattress stitch/ladder stitch

This seam is worked on the right side.

Thread your blunt-ended needle with a length of yarn and
make it secure at the top or at the bottom of the seam on one
side only, by taking one or two small back-stitches neatly on
top of each other.

Before you begin to sew, look at the diagrams overleaf.

Can you see that on both sides the needle stays inside the edge
stitch?

It doesn't matter whether you work up or down the seam. First
lift two threads between the edge stitch and the next, just as the
first diagram shows.

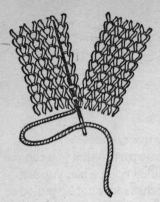

Then take the needle across to the other side, and do the same thing there.

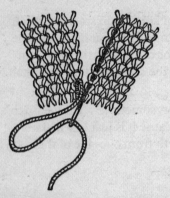

Back to the first side, and lift the next two threads; then across to the other side and repeat that.

Work in this way all up or down the seam, making certain that the stitches you have made are pulled tight. Remember that 'tight' means you can't pull the work apart, but it *doesn't* mean making the seam shorter than the knitting.

Knitting trims
There are several things that are very useful to help give the finishing touches to your knitting. Blanket-stitch can make an attractive edging for certain things, as can fringing. Pompons and tassels, too, are easy to make and very decorative.

Blanket-stitch

This is easy to work as an edging. Look carefully at the diagram to see how it is done, and try to keep the stitches as even as possible.

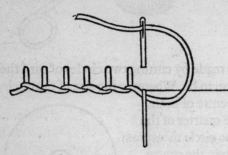

Pompons

Tiny pompons can be made by winding the yarn fairly thickly round two fingers. Don't wind it so tight that you

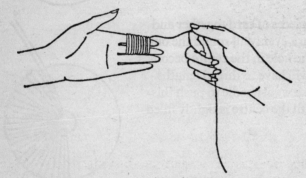

can't get your fingers out, but slip them out carefully and cut the yarn off. Tie this bundle tightly round the centre with a strand of yarn.

Then snip through the loops
and tease them out into a
circle. Trim off any ends that
spoil the shape.

A larger pompon can be made by cutting two circles of card the
size you want the pompon to be. Whatever the size of the circle,
cut a round hole in the centre of both
pieces that measures one quarter of the
complete diameter. If the circle measures
4 cm across, then the gap in the centre
should measure 1 cm.

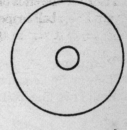

Hold both pieces of card together and
wind the yarn evenly all round the outer
circle. As the hole in the centre becomes
filled, you will have to thread lengths
of yarn into a wool needle to push this
through until the centre is tightly filled.

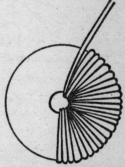

Using the tips of
your scissors, cut
the yarn all round
the outside between
the two card circles.

Twist a strand of yarn
two or three times round the core
of yarn at the centre of the card
circles and tie the ends of this
strand very tightly. Then
remove the card circles.

Tease out the ends of the
yarn into a ball shape and trim
off any that tend to spoil the
outline.

Fringing

The easiest way to make a fringe is to use a crochet hook to
draw the ends of yarn through the edge where the fringe is to be.

Cut several lengths of yarn just over twice the length you want
the finished fringe to be. The number of strands that you put
in each group depends on how much yarn you have to spare
and how thick you want the fringe to be. Take four lengths of
yarn together (or whatever number you have decided on) and
fold them in half.

Put the crochet hook through the edge of the knitting; catch the folded loop in the hook and draw it through the edge.

Then, using the hook again, pull the ends of the fringe through the loop you have made and draw them up tight.

After making a fringe, always trim the ends so that the edge is neat and even.

Tassels

To make a tassel, cut a piece of card the depth you want the tassel to be.

Wind the yarn a number of times round this and then cut the yarn, leaving an end which you can thread into a wool needle.

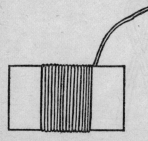

Slip the needle through all the loops at the top of the card and then back through a second time; now stitch it firmly so that it will hold all the loops tightly in place. Pull the

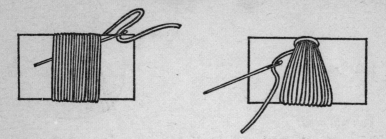

card out and cut through all the loops at the lower edge (unless you want to leave them joined). If you do cut the ends, trim them so that they hang evenly.

12 Things galore

Barbapapa

You will need:
1 (50-g) ball of Patons Double Knitting or Patons Trident
Double Knitting
1 pair of No 8 needles
Kapok, foam or clean chopped-up nylons or tights for stuffing
A little black yarn for eyelashes
2 small pieces of white felt for eyes

Tension: 22 sts to 10 cm measured over St st using Double
Knitting

To work Barbapapa
Body and head
Using No 8 needles and Double Knitting, cast on 13 sts.

Purl 1 row.
2nd row K2, * M1, K1, rep from * until 1 st is left, K1.
Purl 1 row. (You should have 23 sts.)
4th row K1, * M1, K2, rep from * to end.
Purl 1 row. (You should have 34 sts.)
6th row K1, * M1, K3, rep from * to end.
Purl 1 row. (You should have 45 sts.)
8th row K1, * M1, K4, rep from * to end.
Purl 1 row. (You should have 56 sts.)
10th row K1, * M1, K5, rep from * to end.
Purl 1 row. (You should have 67 sts.)
12th row K1, * M1, K6, rep from * to end (78 sts).
Work 3 rows St st (that is, P 1 row, K 1 row, P 1 row).
16th row K1, * M1, K7, rep from * to end (89 sts).

Work 3 rows St st.
20th row K1, * M1, K8, rep from * to end (100 sts).
Work 11 rows St st.

Start to shape top
1st row K4, * K2 tog, K8, rep from * until 6 sts rem, K2 tog, K4.
P 1 row (90 sts).
3rd row K3, * K2 tog, K7, rep from * until 6 sts rem, K2 tog, K4.
P 1 row (80 sts).
5th row K3, * K2 tog, K6, rep from * until 5 sts rem, K2 tog, K3
(70 sts).
Work 3 rows St st.
9th row K2, * K2 tog, K5, rep from * until 5 sts rem, K2 tog, K3
(60 sts).
Work 3 rows St st.
13th row K2, * K2 tog, K4, rep from * until 4 sts rem, K2 tog, K2
(50 sts).
Work 5 rows St st.
19th row K2, * K2 tog, K3, rep from * until 3 sts rem, K2 tog, K1
(40 sts).
Work 17 rows St st.

Shape head
1st row * K2 tog, K2, rep from * to end (30 sts).
P 1 row.
3rd row K2, * K2 tog, K2, rep from * to end (23 sts).
P 1 row.
5th row K2, * K2 tog, K1, rep from * to end (16 sts).
P 1 row.
7th row K1, * K2 tog, K1, rep from * to end (11 sts).
Cut a 20-centimetre end of yarn. Thread into wool needle and
through sts still on needle.

Draw up the sts and seam on the right side using an invisible
seam (see Section 11) half-way down the side. Stuff and
complete seam.

Hands
Work 2 hands alike.
Using No 8 needles and Double Knitting, cast on 8 sts.

Beg with a K row, work 4 rows St st.
Next row ★ K2 tog, rep from ★ to end.
Cast off.

Fold hand in half lengthwise and seam all round.
Sew one hand on each side of his body.

Mouth
Using No 8 needles and black, cast on 8 sts. Cast off.
Darn in ends. Sew in position on face.

Nose
Sew 2 black spots in place for his nose.

Eyes
Cut 2 oval pieces of white felt.
Sew them on making a small patch of black – just a few stitches
on top of each other.

Eyebrows
Cut 10 strands of black 5 cm long.
Use 5 strands for one eyebrow and 5 for the other.
Fold each strand in half and draw it through a knitted stitch on
his face just like a tiny fringe (see diagram). Trim eyebrows
shorter when you have got them in place, and brush them
backwards so that they curl slightly.

Baby's slippers

You will need:
1 (25-g) ball of Patons Baby
    Quickerknit Pure Wool
1 pair of No 9 needles
About 60 cm narrow baby ribbon

Measurements: to fit average foot, birth to 3 months
Tension: 26 sts to 10 cm

To work the slippers
Using No 9 needles, cast on 31 sts.

1st row K.
2nd row K1, M1, K14, M1, K1, M1, K14, M1, K1.

K I row.

4th row KI, MI, KI6, MI, KI, MI, KI6, MI, KI.

K I row.

6th row KI, MI, KI8, MI, KI, MI, KI8, MI, KI.

K I row.

8th row KI, MI, K20, MI, KI, MI, K20, MI, KI.

K IO rows.

Shape toe

1st row K5, turn.

K 8 rows on these 5 sts. Cast off.

With right side of work facing, rejoin yarn to next st.

Next row Cast off 6 sts, K to last 11 sts, cast off 6 sts, K4 (5 sts still on needle).

K 8 rows on these 5 sts. Cast off.

With right side of work facing, rejoin yarn to sts still on needle.

Ribbon-slotting row KI, * yon, K2 tog, rep from * to end.

Start cuff

1st row KI, * PI, KI, rep from * to end.

Rep this row 13 times more. Cast off in ribbing (see page 62).

Work 2nd slipper in the same way.

To make up

Neatly seam sole (cast-on edge) and the strips knitted on 5 sts to their cast-off edges. Sew sides of centre to the 6 cast-off sts at each side. Cut ribbon in half, and thread one piece through slots in each slipper, leaving ends to tie.

Baby's mittens

You will need:

1 (25-g) ball of Patons Baby
    Quickerknit Pure Wool

1 pair of No 9 needles

length of narrow baby ribbon

Measurements: about 11 cm long when complete

Tension: 26 sts to 10 cm measured over pattern

To work the mittens

Using No 9 needles, cast on 32 sts.

1st row * K2, P2, rep from * to end.

Rep 1st row 8 times more.

Ribbon-slotting row K2, * yon, K2 tog, rep from * to end.

Next row K.

Begin pattern

1st row K.
2nd row P.
3rd row K.
4th row K.

Rep 1st–4th pattern rows 3 times more, then 1st and 2nd rows of patt once more.

Shape top

1st row * K1, sl1, K1, psso, K10, K2 tog, K1, rep from * once more.
2nd row K.
3rd row * K1, sl1, K1, psso, K8, K2 tog, K1, rep from * once more.
4th row P.
5th row * K1, sl1, K1, psso, K6, K2 tog, K1, rep from * once more.
6th row K.
7th row * K1, sl1, K1, psso, K4, K2 tog, K1, rep from * once more.
Cast off.

Work 2nd mitten in the same way.

To make up

Fold each mitten in half lengthways and seam, using a back-stitch seam on the wrong side or an invisible seam on the right side from the cast-off edge down the side to the cast-on edge.

Using back-stitch on the wrong side, seam across the top.

Cut the ribbon in half and thread a piece through the slots in each mitten, leaving ends to tie.

These mittens should not need pressing.

Baby's bonnet (to match mittens)

You will need:
1 (25-g) ball of Patons Baby
   Quickerknit Pure Wool
1 pair of No 9 needles
Length 2-cm-wide baby ribbon
Measurements: to fit average head, birth to 3 months
Tension: 26 sts to 10 cm measured over pattern

To work the bonnet
Using No 9 needles, cast on 82 sts.

1st row K2, * P2, K2, rep from * to end.
2nd row P2, * K2, P2, rep from * to end.
Rep 1st and 2nd rows once more for edging.

Begin pattern
1st row K.
2nd row K1, P to last st, K1.
3rd row K.
4th row K.
Rep 1st–4th pattern rows 7 times more.

Shape top
1st row K1, * K2 tog, K7, rep from * to end.
2nd row K.
3rd row K1, * K2 tog, K6, rep from * to end.
4th row K.
5th row K1, * K2 tog, K5, rep from * to end.
6th row K.
7th row K1, * K2 tog, K4, rep from * to end.
8th row K.

9th row K1, * K2 tog, K3, rep from * to end.
10th row K.
11th row K1, * K2 tog, K2, rep from * to end.
12th row K.
13th row K1, * K2 tog, K1, rep from * to end.
14th row K.
15th row K1, * K2 tog, rep from * to end.
Cut a tail of yarn at least 20 cm long. Thread into a wool needle and thread it through all the sts still on the needle.

To make up
Draw the sts together on the thread and, using this end, seam the bonnet from the centre of crown to the edge of the shaped section. Use a back-stitch seam on the wrong side or an invisible seam on the right side.

Sew a length of ribbon to each side at the front corners.

This bonnet should not need pressing.

Tea cosy

You will need:
2 (50-g) balls Patons Double Knitting in main shade (A)
1 (50-g) ball of the same type of yarn in contrast (B)
1 pair of No 9 needles and 1 pair of No 8 needles
Measurements: to fit an average 1-litre teapot
Tension: 22 sts to 10 cm measured over pattern

To work the cosy
Using No 9 needles and A, cast on 51 sts.

K 7 rows. Change to No 8 needles for patt.
Cont in patt:
1st row Using A, K.
2nd row Using B, K1, * keeping yb sl1, K1, rep from * to end.
3rd row Using B, P1, * keeping yf sl1, P1, rep from * to end.
4th row Using A, K.
Work from 1st–4th rows until work measures 15 cm from cast-on edge. Break off B.
Complete, using A only and No 9 needles:
Next row K1, * yf, K2 tog, rep from * to end.
K 2 rows.
Next row K1, * K2 tog, rep from * to end.
Rep last row once. Cast off.

Make a 2nd piece in the same way.

To make up
Press both pieces *lightly* under a damp cloth. Join the sides, leaving an opening for spout or handle in the middle of each seam. Use back-stitch on the wrong side or invisible seaming on the right side.

Tie
Using No 8 needles and A, cast on 30 sts. Cast off.
Thread tie through holes and draw top of cosy up. Tie in place.

Place mat

You will need:
1 (50-g) ball of Patons Trident Double Knitting
1 pair of No 8 needles
Measurements: finished mat (when pressed) measures about
    20 cm by 32 cm
Tension: 28 sts to 10 cm, measured over St st

To work the mat
Using No 8 needles and Trident Double Knitting, cast on 43 sts.
K 6 rows.

Now begin border pattern
1st row K.
2nd row K3, P to last 3 sts, K3.
3rd row K3, * K3, P1, K2, rep from * until 4 sts rem, K4.
4th row K3, * P2, K3, P1, rep from * until 4 sts rem, P1, K3.
5th row K3, * K1, P5, rep from * until 4 sts rem, K4.
6th row Work as given for the 4th row.
7th row Work as given for the 3rd row.
8th row Work as given for the 2nd row.
K 4 rows. This completes the border.

Now work the centre section
K 1 row.
Next row K3, P to last 3 sts, K3.
Rep the last 2 rows until the centre section measures 25 cm, ending with a purl-side row.
K 4 rows.
Work rows 1–8 as given for the other border.
K 6 rows. Cast off.

Darn in the ends and press, after pinning out to shape, on the wrong side.

Rag doll

You will need:
1 (50-g) ball of Patons Double Knitting for body (A)
1 (50-g) ball of the same type of yarn in each of two contrasting colours (B and C)
1 (25-g) ball of Patons Baby Quickerknit Pure Wool in white (D)

1 (50-g) ball of Patons Double Knitting for hair
1 pair of No 9 needles and 1 pair of No 8 needles
kapok, foam or clean chopped-up nylons or tights for stuffing
4 small buttons
small piece of elastic
scraps of red, black, white and brown or blue embroidery
  cotton or fine wool for face
Measurements: about 42 cm tall
Tension: 22 sts to 10 cm on No 8 needles measured over St st

To work the doll

Legs
Using No 8 needles and body colour (A), cast on 24 sts.
Beg with a K row, work in St st.
Work 4 rows.
Next row K8, cast off centre 8 sts, K8.

Cont in St st, drawing the yarn tight across the gap made by the cast-off sts in the previous row.
Work 69 rows more. Cast off.

Work a 2nd leg in the same way.

Body and head
Using No 8 needles and A, cast on 20 sts.
Beg with a K row, work 28 rows in St st.

Shape shoulders and neck
Cast off 3 sts at beg of next 4 rows.
Work 6 rows for neck on these 8 sts.

To work face
1st row K1, M1, K1, M1, K4, M1, K1, M1, K1.
P 1 row.
3rd row K1, M1, K10, M1, K1.
Work 11 rows.
15th row K1, K2 tog, K8, K2 tog, K1.
P 1 row.
17th row K1, K2 tog, K6, K2 tog, K1.
P 1 row.
19th row K1, * K2 tog, K1, rep from * to end.
P 1 row.
21st row K1, * K2 tog, rep from * to end. Cast off.

Work 2nd body and face piece in the same way.

Arms
Using No 8 needles and A, cast on 12 sts.
Beg with a K row, work 20 rows in St st.
Next row K2 tog, K to last 2 sts, K2 tog.
Work 3 rows.
Next row *K2 tog, rep from * to end.
Cut the yarn, leaving a 20-cm tail. Thread tail into a wool needle and draw it through the sts on the needle.

Work 2nd arm in the same way.

Shoes
Using No 8 needles and C, cast on 24 sts.

K 6 rows. Cast off. Work 2nd shoe in same way.

Front flap of shoe

Using No 8 needles and C, cast on 6 sts.

K 4 rows. Cast off. Knit a 2nd flap in the same way.

Skirt

Using No 8 needles and B, cast on 40 sts.

K 4 rows.

Joining in colours as required, K 2 rows C, 2 rows B, 2 rows D, 2 rows B, 2 rows C, 2 rows B, 2 rows D, 2 rows B, 2 rows C.
Break off C and D.

Continue using B only.

K 8 rows.

Shape waist

1st row K1, * K2 tog, rep from * to last st, K1.

K 7 rows for waistband. Cast off.

Straps for skirt

Using No 8 needles and B, cast on 25 sts.

K 3 rows. Cast off. Work 2nd strap in same way.

Shirt

Using No 8 needles and C, cast on 24 sts.

1st row * K1, P1, rep from * to end.

Rep 1st row 7 times more.

Next row Cast on 8 sts, work rest of row in rib as before.

Next row Cast on 8 sts, rib to end.

Work 10 rows. Cast off in rib.

Work 2nd piece in same way.

Pants

Using No 9 needles and D, cast on 44 sts.

K 2 rows.

Cont in St st, beg with a K row.

Work 20 rows.

Work holes for elastic

Next row K2, * yf, K2 tog, rep from * to end.

Work 2 rows in K1, P1 rib.

Cast off.

Scarf

Using No 9 needles and B, cast on 80 sts.

Joining in the colours as required, K 1 row B, 2 rows C, 2 rows D, 2 rows C, 1 row B. Cast off.

Sew a small tassel to each end of the scarf, after darning in the ends.

To make up

Seam legs, arms and body, leaving a small part of one seam of each piece open to stuff. Stuff each section and finish the seam. Sew legs to base of body and arms to each side of shoulders.

Shoes

Fold in half and seam along back and cast-on edge. Sew 2 sts on either side of centre front of upper edge together. Sew flap to centre front over the sts sewn together. Finish the front with a tiny pompon of C.

Pants

Fold in half and seam into a circle. Catch the centres of the lower edge together in the middle to form two 'legs'.

Thread elastic through the waist holes and sew the ends together to form a circle.

Skirt

Fold in half and seam.

Sew one strap to either side both front and back. Finish the ends of the straps at the front with two buttons.

Shirt

Join the two sections together up the sides and along the edge of the cast-on sts which form the sleeves. Seam the shoulders, leaving plenty of room to get it over doll's head.

Hair

Cut about 48 lengths of wool for hair about 40 cm long and stitch them to the doll's head from centre front to centre back. The stitching will look like a parting in the hair. Draw the hair back into bunches or plait and tie with one of the yarn colours.

Embroider mouth, eyes and eyebrows.

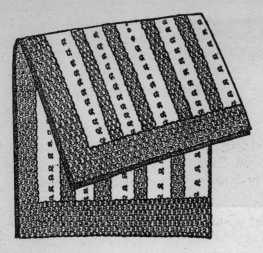

Pram rug

You will need:
4 (50-g) balls of Patons Doublet
1 pair of No 5 needles
Measurements: 47 cm by 60 cm
Tension: 17 sts to 10 cm over St st

To work the rug
Using No 5 needles, cast on 79 sts.

1st row K1, * P1, K1, rep from * to end.
Rep 1st row 10 times more.

Begin pattern
1st row K1 (P1, K1) 3 times, P to last 7 sts, K1 (P1, K1) 3 times.
2nd row K1 (P1, K1) 3 times, K to last 7 sts, K1 (P1, K1) 3 times.
3rd row K1 (P1, K1) 3 times, P to last 7 sts, K1 (P1, K1) 3 times.
4th row K1, * P1, K1, rep from * to end.
5th, 6th, 7th rows Work as for 1st, 2nd and 3rd pattern rows.
8th–12th rows Work as for the 4th pattern row.
Rep 1st–12th rows 10 times more, then rep the 4th pattern row
6 times more. Cast off in moss st.

Finish off ends by darning in neatly. Press very lightly under a
damp cloth.

Cushion

You will need:
2 (50-g) balls Patons Double Knitting in main shade (A)
2 (50-g) balls of the same type of yarn in 1st contrast (B)
1 (50-g) ball of the same type of yarn in 2nd contrast (C)
1 pair of No 8 needles
1 cushion pad 26 cm square
Measurements: each square measures about 13 cm. Four joined together make a cushion front 26 cm square. If you want to cover a cushion completely, you will need to make two pieces, one for the back and one for the front. (Larger cushions can be made by joining more than 4 squares.)
Tension: 9 sts to 4 cm.

To work a square
Using No 8 needles and A, cast on 3 sts.

K 2 rows.
3rd row KI, MI, KI, MI, KI.
K I row.
5th row KI, MI, K3, MI, KI.
K I row.
7th row KI, MI, K5, MI, KI.
K I row.
9th row KI, MI, K7, MI, KI.

104

K I row.

11th row K1, M1, K9, M1, K1.

K I row.

Cont in this way, inc 1 st as before at each end of every alternate row until there are 37 sts. K 1 row.

Next row Using B, K1, M1, K35, M1, K1. K 1 row.

Next row Using B, K2 tog, K35, K2 tog. Using C, K 1 row.

Next row Using C, K2 tog, K33, K2 tog. Using B, K 1 row.

Next row Using B, K2 tog, K31, K2 tog. Using B, K 1 row.

Next row Using A, K2 tog, K29, K2 tog. Using A, K 1 row. Break off A.

Next row Using B, K2 tog, K27, K2 tog. Using B, K 1 row.

Next row Using B, K2 tog, K25, K2 tog. Using C, K 1 row.

Next row Using C, K2 tog, K23, K2 tog. Break off C. Using B, K 1 row.

Cont, using B and dec 1 st at each end of the next and every alt row, until 15 sts rem.

Next row Using B, K2 tog, K11, K2 tog. Break off B. Using C, K 1 row.

Complete using C, cont dec 1 st at each end of next and every alt row as before until 3 sts rem. K 1 row. Cast off.

Work as many squares as are needed.

Darn in all the ends on the wrong side, and join the squares together neatly on the wrong side with back-stitch.

This should not need pressing, but if you decide to press it, do so lightly, without flattening the stitches at all.

Fair Isle banded mittens

You will need:
1 (50-g) ball of Patons Double Knitting in main shade (A)
1 (50-g) ball of each of 2 contrasting shades (B and C)
1 pair of No 8 needles
Measurements: width around hand 17 cm; length to top 20 cm
Tension: 22 sts to 10 cm over St st

To make right-hand mitten
Using No 8 needles and main shade (A), cast on 36 sts.

1st row * K2, P2, rep from * to end.

Rep 1st row 13 times more.

Cont in St st, beg with a K row.

Work 4 rows.

Shape thumb

1st row K19, M1, K17.

P 1 row.

3rd row K19, M1, K1, M1, K17.

P 1 row.

5th row K19, M1, K3, M1, K17.

P 1 row.

7th row K19, M1, K5, M1, K17.

P 1 row.

9th row K19, M1, K7, M1, K17.

P 1 row.

Next row K28 sts, turn.

Next row P9 sts, turn.

***Next row Cast on 3 sts, K the newly cast-on sts and the next 9 sts (12 sts altogether).

Work 7 rows on these 12 sts for the thumb.

Next row * K2 tog, K1, rep from * to end. P 1 row.

Next row * K2 tog, rep from * to end.

Cut the yarn, leaving a 20-cm tail and thread through the rem sts.

With right side of work facing, rejoin the yarn to the sts to the left of the thumb.

1st row Cast on 3 sts, K across the newly cast-on sts, then across the 17 sts on the left-hand needle (20 sts).

2nd row P across these 20 sts and then on across the other 19 sts the other side of the thumb (39 sts).

Work Fair Isle pattern
1st row K1A, * 1B, 3A, until 2 sts rem, 1B, 1A. Break off B.
2nd row Using A, P.
3rd row K3A, * 1C, 3A, rep from * to end.
4th row P1C, * 1A, 1C, rep from * to end.
5th row As 3rd. Break off C.
6th row Using A, P.
7th row Rejoin B. Work as 1st row. Break off B.
Using A only, work 9 rows in St st, beg with a P row.

Shape top
1st row K1, * sl1, K1, psso, K14, K2 tog, K1, rep from * once more.
P 1 row.
3rd row K1, * sl1, K1, psso, K12, K2 tog, K1, rep from * once more.
P 1 row.
5th row K1, * sl1, K1, psso, K10, K2 tog, K1, rep from * once more.
P 1 row.
7th row K1, * sl1, K1, psso, K8, K2 tog, K1, rep from * once more.
P 1 row.
9th row K1, * sl1, K1, psso, K6, K2 tog, K1, rep from * once more.
Cast off.

To work left-hand mitten
Work the ribbing in the same way as for the right mitten.
Work 4 rows in St st, beg with a K row.

Shape thumb
1st row K17, M1, K19.
P 1 row.
3rd row K17, M1, K1, M1, K19.
P 1 row.
5th row K17, M1, K3, M1, K19.

P 1 row.

7th row K17, M1, K5, M1, K19.

P 1 row.

9th row K17, M1, K7, M1, K19.

P 1 row.

Next row K26, turn.

Next row P9 sts, turn.

Work the thumb as given for the other mitten from *** to end of thumb, and then rejoin the yarn to the group of 19 sts to the left of the completed thumb.

Next row Cast on 3 sts, K all 22 sts.

Next row P all 39 sts.

Complete as for the other hand.

To make up

Seam each mitten along the cast-off edge and down the side to the start of the ribbing.

Seam the thumb from the tip to the cast-on sts and then join (as neatly as possible) the two sets of cast-on sts together.

Press each mitten under a damp cloth with a warm iron, being careful *not* to press the ribbing of the cuff.

Lacy apron

You will need:

2 (25-g) balls of Patons Baby Courtelle 4 ply

1 pair of No 9 needles

Measurements: apron section measures 30 cm wide and 25 cm deep before gathering on to band

Tension: 20 sts to 10 cm measured over lace pattern

To work the apron

Using No 9 needles, cast on 56 sts.

K 8 rows.

Begin lace pattern

1st row K4, * K1, yf, yrn, P2 tog, K1, rep from * to last 4 sts, K4.

Rep 1st row until work measures 25 cm.

Cast off.

Waistband

Using No 9 needles, cast on 6 sts.

K every row until strip is long enough to tie around your waist.

If this seems very long, make the strip just 5 cm longer than your waist measurement and sew a very small piece of Velcro fastener to either end to close it and keep the apron in place.

To make up

Gather the top edge (cast-off edge) on to the edge of the waistband. Press *very lightly* under a damp cloth with a warm iron. This pattern needs no pressure at all when you press it.

Chevron striped bag

You will need:
1 (50-g) ball of Patons Double Knitting in each of main shade (A), first contrasting colour (B) and second contrast (C)
1 pair of No 8 needles
8 small curtain rings

Measurements: about 23 cm square
Tension: one pattern of 14 sts measures about 6 cm

To work the bag

Using No 8 needles and A, cast on 57 sts.

K 2 rows.

Begin pattern

1st row Using B, K1, * M1, K4, K2 tog, K1, sl1, K1, psso, K4, M1, K1, rep from * to end.

2nd row Using B, P.

3rd row As 1st row.

4th row Using B, P.

5th row Using C, work as for 1st row.

6th row Using C, K.

7th row Using C, work as for 1st row.

8th row Using C, P.

9th row Using B, work as for 1st row.

10th row Using B, P.

11th row Using A, work as for 1st row.

12th row Using A, K.

Rep 1st–12th rows 4 times more.

Cast off.

Work a 2nd piece in the same way.

Strap

Using No 8 needles and A, cast on 8 sts.

K every row until strap is as long as required – about 50 cm. Fold in half lengthwise and sew the edges together.

Make a second strap in the same way.

To make up

Press each section lightly under a damp cloth with a warm iron.

On the wrong side, join cast-on edges and side seams.

Choose one of the colours to work blanket-stitch to cover the curtain rings. Sew one ring to the tip of each peak around the top edge.

Thread one strap through all the rings and sew into a circle, and then sew the other strap in the same way so that one string may be pulled up in either direction to close the top of the bag.

You can make a small tassel or pompon to sew to the tip of every peak on the bottom edge.

Bedroom slippers

You will need:
2 (50-g) balls Patons Doublet
1 pair of No 5 needles
1.30 m narrow ribbon
Measurements: to fit a 15–20-cm foot
Tension: approx. 8 sts to 5 cm over stretched-out ribbing

To work slippers

Using No 5 needles, cast on 58 sts.

1st row K2, * P2, K2, rep from * to end.
2nd row P2, * K2, P2, rep from * to end.

Rep 1st and 2nd rows until work measures 16 cm.

Work ribbon-slotting row P2, * yon, K2 tog, rep from * to end.
Work 1 row rib.

Work cuff
1st row Cast off 13, rib to end.
2nd row Cast off 13, K to end.
K 10 rows.
Cast off.

Work 2nd slipper in the same way.

To make up
Fold slipper in half and seam down centre front and along the cast-on edge for the sole.

Thread ribbon through slotting to tie at centre front, or make a tie by casting on 80 sts, and casting off at once (not too tightly).

Thread through the holes, beginning and ending at centre front. Make 4 small tassels or pompons and sew one to each end of the ties.